THE YOUNG INVESTIGATOR'S GUIDE TO

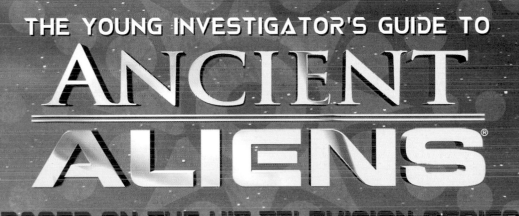

ANCIENT ALIENS®

BASED ON THE HIT TELEVISION SERIES

THE YOUNG INVESTIGATOR'S GUIDE TO

ANCIENT ALIENS®

BASED ON THE HIT TELEVISION SERIES

 ROARING BROOK PRESS
NEW YORK

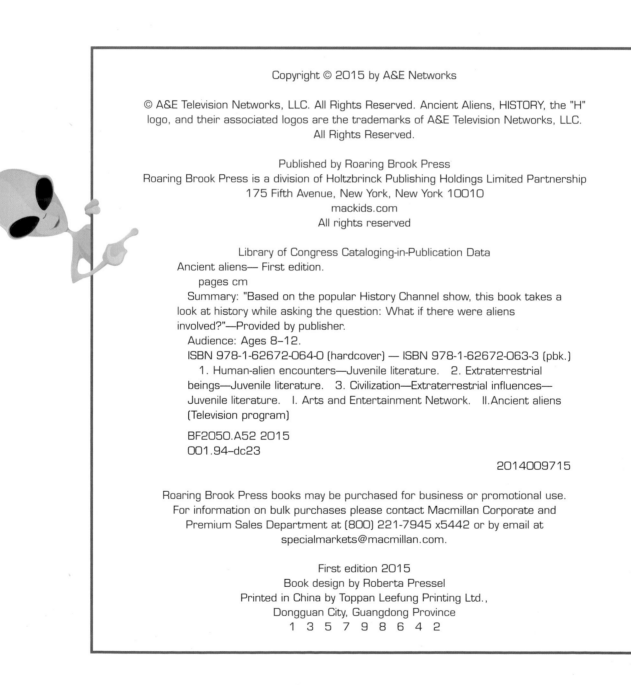

Published by Roaring Brook Press
Roaring Brook Press is a division of Holtzbrinck Publishing Holdings Limited Partnership
175 Fifth Avenue, New York, New York 10010
mackids.com
All rights reserved

Library of Congress Cataloging-in-Publication Data
Ancient aliens— First edition.
        pages cm
    Summary: "Based on the popular History Channel show, this book takes a
look at history while asking the question: What if there were aliens
involved?"—Provided by publisher.
    Audience: Ages 8–12.
    ISBN 978-1-62672-064-0 (hardcover) — ISBN 978-1-62672-063-3 (pbk.)
        1. Human-alien encounters—Juvenile literature.   2. Extraterrestrial
beings—Juvenile literature.   3. Civilization—Extraterrestrial influences—
Juvenile literature.   I. Arts and Entertainment Network.   II.Ancient aliens
(Television program)
    BF2050.A52 2015
    001.94–dc23

                                                                            2014009715

Roaring Brook Press books may be purchased for business or promotional use.
For information on bulk purchases please contact Macmillan Corporate and
Premium Sales Department at (800) 221-7945 x5442 or by email at
specialmarkets@macmillan.com.

First edition 2015
Book design by Roberta Pressel
Printed in China by Toppan Leefung Printing Ltd.,
Dongguan City, Guangdong Province
1 3 5 7 9 8 6 4 2

CONTENTS

INTRODUCTION:

ANCIENT ALIENS— EXPLAINING THE THEORY

On July 20, 1969, the *Apollo 11* space mission reached its destination, and the astronauts who had traveled 238,900 miles from Earth stepped onto the surface of the moon. Mission commander Neil Armstrong proclaimed the moon landing a "giant leap for mankind," and it certainly was. It was the first time in history that beings left their home planet and traveled through space to stand on another world.

Or was it?

Were we really the first creatures in the universe capable of traveling to a distant celestial body—in 1969? The universe is extraordinarily old. Scientists believe it was formed between 13 and 20 billion years ago by an enormous burst of energy known as the Big Bang. Astronomers know there are billions, maybe even trillions, of stars and planets out there. In 2013, an analysis of data from NASA's Kepler space telescope determined that there could be 40 billion habitable, Earth-size planets in our own galaxy. *Habitable* means they might contain or have the right mix of chemical and environmental elements to contain life. Some of that life could merely be microscopic organisms. Some might be more advanced than we are.

Millions of people around the world believe we have been visited in the past by extraterrestrial beings. What if it were true? Did ancient aliens really help to shape our history?

The television show *Ancient Aliens* has spent years examining the possibility that aliens did in fact visit Earth in distant times, and they left clues. All around the globe are incredible ancient structures—like the Pyramids in Egypt, Puma Punku in Bolivia, Stonehenge in England—apparently constructed to align with objects in space, yet their construction remains a mystery. It's unknown how ancient people with primitive tools could precisely engineer, cut, and move stones weighing literally hundreds of tons. Ancient Astronaut theorists study the possibility of human interaction with extraterrestrials over the course of thousands of years. They look at evidence including artifacts, ancient texts, ruins, and other structures to hypothesize about the role of aliens in specific moments in history. A major text in the field of Ancient Astronaut theory is a book called *Chariots of the Gods*, by Erich von Däniken, published in 1968. In this book, von Däniken outlines many hypotheses about the possible historical connections between humans and extraterrestrials. Ancient Astronaut theorists have expanded on von Däniken's work as they research specific time periods in world history.

Primitive cultures from around the world have left illustrations and sculptures that seem to depict otherworldly beings, some of whom appear to be wearing spacesuits and helmets. And many ancient cultures have left us stories of beings who came down from the sky. Among these stories there are tales of visits from "star people" and "sky people," who were credited with creating the universe or starting mankind. The ancient cultures often worshipped them as gods.

The Great Pyramids of Giza

El Castillo at Chichen Itza

One basic principle of Ancient Astronaut theory is that primitive cultures exposed to technology vastly more advanced than their own might misinterpret the technology as magic. And they might think of the beings who control the magic as wizards—or even gods. Science and science fiction writer Arthur C. Clarke famously wrote: "Any sufficiently advanced technology is indistinguishable from magic." Imagine showing something like an iPhone, or a television set, or a rifle to a Stone Age tribe. What would they think about you and your mysterious power? Cases exist from not so long ago, when remote people on islands in the South Pacific were exposed to modern technology and weapons during World War II. Some of them even believed their visitors to be worthy of worship.

The tombstone of King Pakal from the Temple of the Inscriptions. Many believe the images engraved on the top depict ancient extraterrestrial activity.

Ancient texts from cultures all over the world contain references to beings who came from the sky. The Mayans of Central America, who had extremely advanced astronomical knowledge for their time, have texts known as the Chilam Balam which say that **"the road to the stars descended from the sky, and the 13 and 9 gods came to Earth."**

"Can it be more clear?" asks Ancient Astronaut expert Giorgio Tsoukalos, whose face (and gravity-defying hairstyle) is familiar to anyone who has watched the *Ancient Aliens* television show. "Right there we have a direct reference to someone that has arrived from outer space, and we have a written record about this."

Even the Bible, in the Old Testament book of Ezekiel, describes a fiery vessel carrying beings who arrive from above: "Then I looked, and behold, a whirlwind was coming out of the north, a great cloud with raging fire engulfing itself; and brightness was all around it and radiating out of its midst like the color of amber, out of the midst of the fire. Also from within it came the likeness of four living creatures."

Another basic idea of Ancient Aliens theory is that when early cultures developed the ability to write—to record their knowledge for eternity—the first things they took the effort to chisel into stone weren't made-up fantasy stories. They wrote down information they believed to be true, information they felt that others needed to know, based on events they had witnessed or learned about. Is it really possible that every ancient story of beings or gods coming from the sky was purely imagined?

Some ask why, if aliens ever did visit Earth, aren't we seeing them now. In fact, scientists refer to something called the Fermi Paradox. In 1950, the physicist **Enrico Fermi** asked, if extraterrestrial civilizations supposedly exist throughout our galaxy, why haven't we seen any traces of them in modern times?

One answer to that question is that Earth has been around for about 4.6 billion years, and modern human beings have existed for an estimated 200,000 years, yet we have been keeping modern records of what has occurred on our planet for only about 5,000 years.

Enrico Fermi

Concluding that there have never been any aliens, just because we haven't seen them recently, would be like watching one or two pitches of a baseball game and deciding there's no such thing as a home run because nobody hit one while you were watching.

We are fortunate to live in an incredible time right now. There is so much we know about the world. And yet there is so much we still don't know. For the curious, the adventurous, the smart, there are still wondrous mysteries to be solved, science to be tested, and history to be uncovered. Where did we come from? How far back does the world go? What's really out there in space? Beneath our oceans? In distant lands across the globe? Even in our own backyards? Whether you believe in aliens or not, the questions remain. The quest to understand where we came from is a question that crosses from folklore and religion into archaeology, biology, and all the most advanced sciences we have.

The whole concept of ancient aliens certainly has some people frightened, though not necessarily scared of what aliens might do. Some theories believe they're friendly. The scarier implication may be this: if aliens ever do show up, it will change everything. **What we think we know about humanity's past could be completely wrong.**

TIMELINE OF SPACE AND CIVILIZATION

4.6 TO 4.4 BILLION YEARS AGO
Earth is formed.

Primitive agriculture and farming begin.

In ancient Egypt, the pyramids of Giza are constructed, aligned with stars.

13 TO 20 BILLION YEARS AGO
The Big Bang creates the universe.

200,000 YEARS AGO
Modern *homo sapiens* (people) evolve on Earth.

c. 4500 BC
In Carnac, France, more than 3,000 stones are arranged, possibly as astronomical markers.

1800 BC TO 1697 AD
The Mayans, inhabiting areas of present day Central America, develop detailed astronomical tables to predict the movement of the sun, moon, Venus, and other planets.

c. 3000 BC
Stonehenge, a mysterious stone structure that may have been a primitive calendar, aligned to stars and planets, is erected in England.

21,000 YEARS AGO
During the last ice age, the Bering Land Bridge links Asia to Alaska, allowing the first humans into North America.

4.6 BILLION YEARS AGO
Our solar system is formed.

350 BC
Ancient Greek philosophers and mathematicians figure out that Earth is round.

65 MILLION YEARS AGO
Mass extinction of the dinosaurs, possibly caused by an asteroid smashing into Earth.

c. 4000 BC TO 3500 BC
Ancient Sumerians build the world's first cities in Mesopotamia, an area called the "cradle of civilization." Today this area is known as Iraq. Sumerians use metal tools and weapons, create the earliest writing system, and keep records of the sun, moon, and planets.

c. 600 AD
The precision-carved blocks of Puma Punku in Bolivia are put together (possibly much earlier than this date).

Polish astronomer and mathematician Nicolaus Copernicus suggests that the sun—not Earth—is at the center of the universe. The theory that puts the sun in the middle is called "heliocentric."

1923
Astronomer Edwin Hubble shows that other galaxies exist outside the Milky Way.

Chariots of the Gods by Erich von Däniken is published. In this book, many of the principles of Ancient Astronaut theory are described by von Däniken.

2009
NASA launches the Kepler space telescope with the mission to seek Earthlike planets outside our solar system. In November 2013, a report based on Kepler-gathered data indicates that there could be 40 billion habitable Earthlike planets in our galaxy.

1700s
English Astronomer Edmond Halley correctly predicts the time when a comet will return to our sky. It comes to be called Halley's Comet.

1958
President Dwight D. Eisenhower signs the National Aeronautics and Space Act, forming NASA.

1990
NASA launches the Hubble space telescope to get a better look at outer space. Images that Hubble has beamed back to Earth have helped astronomers determine the age of the universe and understand how galaxies and stars evolve.

1600s
Johannes Kepler develops accurate theories about how planets orbit around the sun.
Galileo Galilei builds telescopes that can look deeper into space.
Isaac Newton's *Philosphiae Naturalis Principia Mathematica* describes laws of gravity.

1500s
Ceres is the first asteroid discovered.

1926
Physicist Robert Goddard pioneers the first use of liquid rocket fuel.

1960s
Early work on SETI, the search for extraterrestrial intelligence, is conducted using radio transmitters and receivers to seek communication with beings beyond Earth. The SETI Institute in California is founded in 1984.

1969
Astronauts Neil Armstrong and Buzz Aldrin are the first humans to walk on the moon.

1998
The NASA Astrobiology Institute is created to study how life evolves in the universe and to explore whether there is life beyond Earth.

2012
Launched the previous year, NASA's Curiosity Rover successfully lands on Mars and begins gathering data about the planet to send back to Earth.

HOW DO WE KNOW WHAT ALIENS LOOK LIKE?

Close your eyes and imagine what a visitor from outer space looks like. What picture comes into your head? You may be imagining a creature with a skinny body, with sticklike arms and long fingers. His or her skin is leathery, and greyish or greenish. The alien has a large head—a seriously large head, like putting an onion or squash on top of a Popsicle stick. **He or she has big, oval eyes—liquidy, black eyes that wrap around the sides of the head a little like sunglasses or goggles.**

Is this the alien you are imagining? It's the way a lot of people picture space aliens.

Where does that picture come from? Probably from movies or cartoons, right? It's one of the most popular ways to depict an extraterrestrial. But where did movies and cartoons get their visions of aliens? The fact is that all around the world, going back centuries, drawings and sculptures have been found that depict beings who don't look like anybody that comes from this planet. Many resemble what we, today, might see as a picture of a visitor from outer space.

Those big-headed, leathery-skinned aliens are known to UFO researchers as the "Greys." Similar descriptions of them have come up in multiple accounts of alien encounters from ancient and modern times.

Recent descriptions seem to match ancient depictions of so-called sky gods and star people. But how could ancient descriptions look similar if they are from a time when human civilizations around the globe were separate from each other with no way of communicating? Might they be from the same race of otherworldly visitors—as Ancient Astronauts theorists believe? Here's a gallery of pictures and sculptures from around the globe depicting what might really be ancient aliens.

Petroglyphs in Sego Canyon Utah, USA (circa 2,000 BC)

Ancient Aztec figurine
(circa 1,300 to 1,500 AD)

Dogu statue from Japan (circa 1,000 to 250 BC)

Alabaster figure from Tel Brak, Syria
(circa 3,500 to 3,300 BC)

Aboriginal rock art (circa 3,800 BC)

WHERE DID ANCIENT ALIENS COME FROM?

If aliens did in fact come to Earth, they had to come from somewhere. Their arrival would not only prove that life exists on other planets, but that there are and have been civilizations vastly more advanced or equally as complex as ours. The idea that life may exist on other planets isn't science fiction. It's modern science. Astronomers are exploring the possibility of extraterrestrial life right now, and they're learning more every day.

EVIDENCE OF LIFE IN THE UNIVERSE

The search to define and find life in space is a science called astrobiology or exobiology. It's the fastest-growing branch of astronomy right now. In 2009, America's space agency NASA launched the Kepler space telescope with a mission to seek Earthlike planets outside our solar system. The scientists were searching for the possible existence of planets in what is called the "Goldilocks zone." The Goldilocks zone is an area in a galaxy that is the perfect distance away from a star, meaning not too hot and not too cold—just right. A planet in the Goldilocks zone has the best chance of maintaining a climate that could make a comfortable home for life.

By November 2013, a report based on Kepler data indicated that there could be 40 billion habitable Earthlike planets in our galaxy. *Forty billion.* The *New York Times* reported that astronomers determined "one out of every five sun-like stars in the galaxy has a planet the size of Earth circling it in the Goldilocks zone." And the more similar to Earth a planet is, the higher the chance that life there would be similar to us.

In 2017, NASA is scheduled to launch the Transiting Exoplanet Survey Satellite, nicknamed TESS, which may provide a closer look at a planet just like Earth. This idea is sometimes referred to as Earth 2.0.

Closer to home, NASA has conducted many missions to explore both the moon and Mars. Evidence of water was found on Mars in 2008. In 2011, scientists with NASA's Jet Propulsion Laboratory launched the Mars Science Laboratory. It carried a one-ton, car-sized robot rover named Curiosity designed to probe the Red Planet's surface. One of the reasons they launched Curiosity was to see if Mars is, or ever was, able to support life. Like NASA's space telescopes, Curiosity has been sending amazing images and video back to Earth that anyone can watch online.

An artistic representation of our solar system

But is NASA really sharing all that it has discovered about the universe? Or, as Ancient Aliens theorists suggest, is NASA protecting us from part of the truth? Some claim that NASA knows more than it is telling the public. If aliens ever did make contact with Earth, information being kept confidential may hold clues to where those aliens came from.

THE NASA CONNECTION

Some researchers point to the original moon landing, the *Apollo 11* mission in 1969. More than two hours of video released from that mission shows astronauts Neil Armstrong and Buzz Aldrin making humankind's historic first walk on the surface of the moon. The space pioneers collected rock samples, took photos, and planted an American flag in the lunar soil.

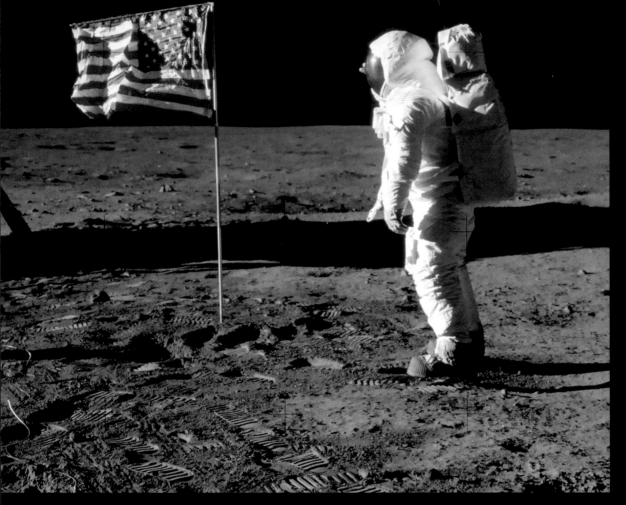

Astronaut Neil Armstrong is the first human to walk on the moon.

But did the astronauts do other things away from the camera that were kept secret? Some theorists believe that the American explorers weren't just collecting rocks, but may have also made discoveries that are still not public today. They also suggest that the "Space Race" of the 1950s and 1960s, a tense contest between the United States and the Soviet Union to see which superpower nation would get its astronauts to the moon first, was a time when the full story behind these space missions was kept under wraps. After all, some theorists point out that when NASA was created in 1958, it was established as part of the country's Department of Defense, which meant that its findings could be classified as top secret. Why would discoveries on the moon or other planets need to be kept secret?

In 1960, NASA worked with a respected Washington research firm called the Brookings Institution to create what was called The Brookings Report. Within this report was a section discussing "the implications of a discovery of extraterrestrial life." It's clear that the quest to learn more about the unknown may have been an important component of the Space Race.

ASTRONAUT ENCOUNTERS WITH ETs

Astronauts on several space missions have reported experiencing encounters with celestial entities that remain unexplained.

In 1991, the space shuttle *Discovery* STS-48 flew nearly 350 miles above Earth, with a mission including deployment of an Upper Atmosphere Research Satellite. A number of amateurs who were directly monitoring the transmissions have produced what they allege is genuine footage from STS-48. The video shows what appears to be a series of unidentified glowing objects and flashing lights that change direction and accelerate rapidly.

According to Michael Bara, co-author of *Dark Mission: The Secret History of NASA*, with Richard C. Hoaglund, one of the astronauts openly stated, **"Hey, we're being tracked by an alien spacecraft."**

"And then all of a sudden the transmission just ceases," Bara says. "I think what happened was that he must have realized he was on the public channel, not the private channel, and he probably very, very quickly switched over to the private channel to describe what it was he was

Astronauts Neil Armstrong, Michael Collins, and Edward "Buzz" Aldrin are the first people to successfully travel to the moon and back.

seeing." Bara claims that video from two shuttle missions, STS-48 and STS-80, both show what appear to be powered vehicles in space, operating in ways that defy laws of physics, moving the way that UFOs might.

American astronauts aren't the only space travelers reporting otherworldly encounters. In 1985, Soviet cosmonauts aboard the *Salyut 7* reported seeing seven celestial beings outside the space station. Six cosmonauts claimed that as they looked out the window of the International Space Station, they saw what they described as winged angels surrounding their ship.

Could these sightings be legitimate? Ancient Aliens expert Giorgio Tsoukalos says we need to keep in mind that astronauts are trained scientists:

Ever since humankind launched itself into space, there have been reports where astronauts describe something that they saw while being up in the spaceship. And we have to remind ourselves that those stories are reported by astronauts . . . and not by crazy people.

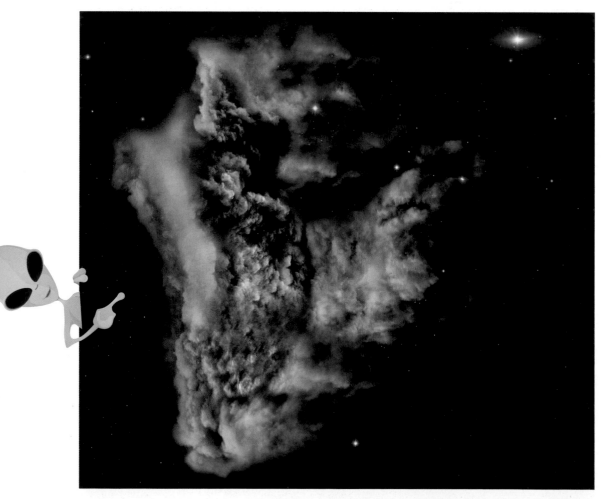

Did Russian cosmonauts see clouds like these outside their spaceship window, or might they have had an extraterrestrial encounter?

ANCIENT ALIEN ENCOUNTERS . . . DOCUMENTED?

One of the key concepts explored in Ancient Astronaut theory is the idea that if early people saw extraterrestrial beings descend from the sky and land on Earth, then their technology and understanding of the universe was not sophisticated enough for them to understand what these beings were. They may have misunderstood the technology they were seeing and described these visitors as angels or gods, and they might have written texts describing these awe-inspiring visitors from the sky as religious figures. The notion that otherworldly beings came to Earth from the heavens is one of the most common themes of ancient mythology and religion. But what were these "gods," really? Do worldwide legends of gods from the sky prove we had a connection with extraterrestrial beings?

Even today, though many of us are taught to believe that God is everywhere, we might look up toward the sky when we are asked where God is. Why do we think God is in the sky? Why is heaven commonly thought to be located up beyond the clouds? One thing we know for sure is that up there is outer space.

In some ancient mythologies, so-called sky gods arrive on Earth in flaming or flying ships.

"The God that I believe in doesn't need a vehicle in which to move around from Point A to Point B," says Ancient Aliens expert Giorgio Tsoukalos.

Some people believe the stories in ancient religious texts are simply parables invented by scholars to teach people lessons. But some researchers think the events described in sacred texts, from cultures throughout time, are based on events that really did happen long ago. A lot of these ancient texts describe occurrences that seem like encounters with beings. Here are some examples.

THE ANUNNAKI OF SUMERIAN MYTHOLOGY

The region that now is the country of Iraq was once known as Mesopotamia, a word that means "between the rivers." This area between the Tigris and Euphrates rivers was home to some of the world's first-known civilizations. The Sumerians are thought to have built some of the first cities. They made advances in agriculture, metalworking, mathematics, and astronomy and developed the first writing system: wedge-shaped markings on clay tablets called cuneiform.

In 1849, 6,000-year-old Sumerian clay tablets containing some of the earliest known forms of written records were discovered. Interpretations of the accounts on these tablets tell the story of a race of ancient beings called the Anunnaki, gods who descended from the sky. "Anunnaki" means "from heaven to Earth they came." Ancient Astronaut theorists say the Sumerians believed the Anunnaki originally came to Earth to mine our planet's gold, but, when the work proved difficult, they bred with the early humans who were already here to create a race of willing workers.

Author Zecharia Sitchin says the Adamu, the first modern human, was created by the Anunnaki 450,000 years ago, when they genetically mixed their DNA with that of prehistoric people.

It's a mind-bending story. It suggests that the first modern human may have been half alien. In essence, the proof that aliens once visited our planet might be in your mirror! The story of Adamu as the first human bears a striking resemblance to the biblical story of creation, where the first man, created by God, was called Adam. Is this just a coincidence, or is it possible that these stories are one and the same?

Did early humans ever look up at the sky and wonder what, or who, else was out there?

SKY WARS OF THE INDIAN GODS

Ancient Sanskrit texts from India dating back as far as 1500 BC describe flying machines called vimanas, piloted by the gods. These aircraft seem similar to airplanes in the way they are described, with many of the modern characteristics of aircraft. Various kinds of vimanas are described in these ancient texts, including some that have flapping wing propulsion systems. But all of these flying machines seem to have characteristics of modern day flight.

Says Giorgio Tsoukalos:

If you read the ancient Indian epics, they read like modern-day science fiction, yet they are thousands of years old, with references not only to flying chariots, and to these gods that had these incredible technological capabilities, but incredible weapons that they used in those epic battles.

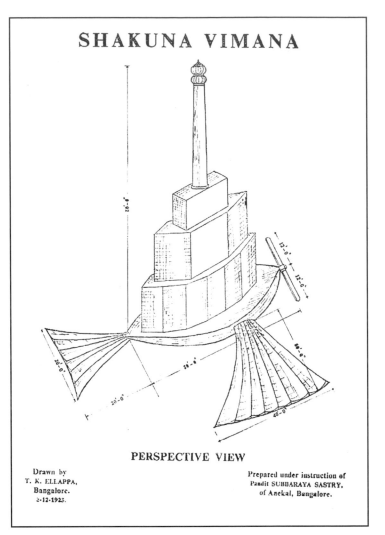

Diagram of an ancient Indian flying machine called a vimana

Did these flying machines and weapons of ancient lore actually exist? And if so, what were they really? One ancient Indian text describes three important giant cities—one was orbiting the Earth, the other was flying in the air, and a third was stationary on the ground. Tsoukalos says those giant cities were often described as being made of gleaming metal and iron. Those three cities went to war with each other, and the gods flung weapons at each other. Were they really "giant cities"? Or could they have been extraterrestrial spacecraft that ancient people struggled to describe because they had never seen anything so *"out of this world"*?

What is it that our ancestors tried to describe here? I think that it was some type of a technology that was witnessed, yet our ancestors, while being highly intelligent, didn't under-stand the nuts and bolts behind that technology. So they created something divine out of it, something supernatural.

NATIVE AMERICANS AND STAR BEINGS

Among the many wonders of time and nature in America's Southwest, you can find ancient drawings called petroglyphs (meaning "stone carvings"). Many of them are on the faces of cliffs in southern Utah on lands where ancestors of the Hopi Indians, the Anasazi, once dwelled. The Anasazi left images scratched into stone. Some appear to depict scenes from everyday life, such as people hunting and animals like longhorn sheep. Other images appear to depict humanlike beings who aren't quite human. And some pictures look something like . . . space-ships. These images support certain Native American myths that tell of "star people" who arrived from above.

Giorgio Tsoukalos says: *"They look like beings with antennae on their heads, or beings that wear some type of a suit . . . They look like depictions of spacemen."*

Prehistoric cave drawings bearing a striking resemblance to common ideas of alien visitors

Both images represent ancient Anasazi rock art and are located in the southwest United States.
Some believe the clothing in these drawings resembles the clothing of space travel.

STRANGE ENCOUNTER IN MEDIEVAL GERMANY

On the morning of April 14, 1561, the citizens of Nuremberg, Germany, awoke to what was described in a local news flier as "a dreadful apparition." Strange objects were spotted in the sky in what appeared to be an aerial battle. Witnesses described flying cigar-shaped objects, circles, or disks hovering in the air, as well as flying crosses. Without the knowledge of modern aircraft technology, could a "flying cross" actually have been an airplane-like machine? Was this an alien encounter that was misinterpreted as a heavenly battle? The scene was illustrated in a newspaper of the time. Is it possible that the people of Nuremberg were actually witnesses to a war between extraterrestrial factions?

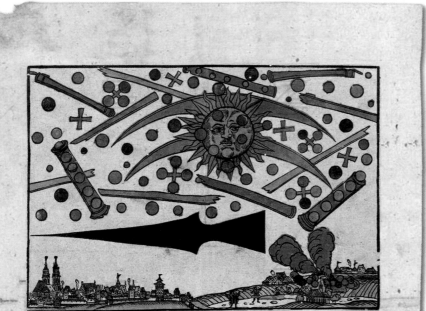

Aerial battle over Nuremberg, Germany, from a sixteenth-century German newspaper

Legendary explorer
Christopher Columbus

CELEBRITY SIGHTING: CHRISTOPHER COLUMBUS

Even **Christopher Columbus** seems to have had an alien sighting, ironically on his way to discover the "New World." Columbus reported it in his log, just days before he reached the shores of America. At about 10 p.m. on October 11, 1492, the explorer was on the deck of the *Santa Maria* when he saw a **light glimmering at a great distance.**

Columbus wrote: "The Admiral, standing on the quarter-deck saw a light. Calling to Pedro Gutierrez, he told him he saw a light, and bid him look that way, which he did and saw it. The Admiral again perceived it once or twice, appearing like the light of a wax candle moving up and down." Summoning another member of the crew, the two watched as the light vanished and reappeared repeatedly. Was this a UFO? What's intriguing is that this likely occurred in what we call the Bermuda Triangle, an area now known for reports of unusual occurrences, including disappearances of ships and planes—and UFO reports.

The biggest unanswered question about ancient aliens traveling from distant planets to Earth is also the simplest: why? We know Earth is a terrific planet—a fine place to live and probably not a bad place to visit. But in a universe with billions of planets, why here?

Why us? Why come all this way? Wasn't there someplace closer?

Experts speculate that the reasons aliens would visit Earth are the same reasons humans have journeyed across our planet: to get things we need, to explore and learn about what's out there, and sometimes to escape where we were. It's possible that ancient aliens would have come here to get something that was in short supply where they lived. One theory says that the substance they sought here was something we've always considered very valuable: gold.

DID ALIENS COME TO MINE OUR GOLD?

The idea that other planets might contain valuable elements that can be mined or harvested isn't science fiction. When American astronauts landed on the moon in 1969, at first it seemed to be a barren landscape of dust and rocks. But later testing determined that the moon's soil contains a high amount of Helium 3, a potentially powerful, nonpolluting, nonradioactive fuel source. An energy source like that, if harnessed, could change the way we live on Earth, maybe help to cure our energy and environmental problems. If the moon—the very closest planetlike orb out there—contains a substance we could use here on Earth, imagine what else lies out in the universe. And, if you can imagine intergalactic travelers from other worlds who have knowledge beyond ours, it's not hard to think that they might be traveling in space to find useful resources. And they might know where to look.

In the 2011 movie *Cowboys and Aliens*, aliens attack a town in the American Old West as part of a mission to extract our gold. But what are the unique properties of gold that might make it worth traveling through the galaxy for?

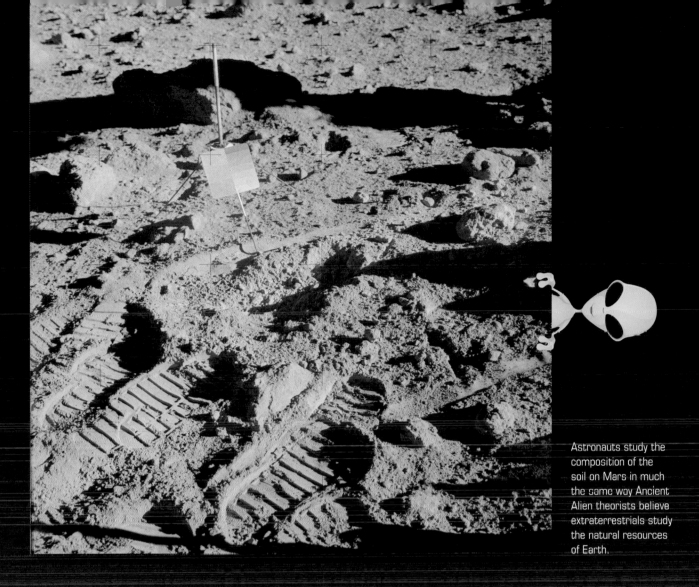

Astronauts study the composition of the soil on Mars in much the same way Ancient Alien theorists believe extraterrestrials study the natural resources of Earth.

Gold, found in the Earth in nuggets and flakes, has been valued since before the days of ancient Egypt, for many reasons. Of course, gold is shiny and lustrous. It was used from the earliest times for decoration and jewelry and medallions. The Egyptians made King Tut's mask of gold and reserved the precious metal for depictions of kings and gods.

In more practical terms, though, gold is a very useful metal. It's easy to mold and reshape. Gold doesn't corrode or rust. It's more or less indestructible. Gold from ancient times still exists today. Gold is also a good conductor of electricity, and because of this, some scientists believe gold may be an asset in the construction of spaceships.

"I think for extraterrestrials, gold would be an important resource just like it is for us," says Michael Dennin, a physicist and professor at the University of California in Irvine. "If it's at all like our society, one of the major things it's going to be built on is electricity, and gold really is one of the top conductors. Its malleability, the ability to make it into wires, use it in really small forms as nanoparticles, is going to make it an incredible technological resource for any sort of life forms which reach that level of dealing with electricity and technology."

We know from history books that American prospectors headed west during the gold rush that started in 1848. Do you think extraterrestrials might have had a gold rush of their own, even before that? Some ancient legends—and some mysterious places around the world—suggest just that.

GOLD DIGGERS OF 3000 BC?

Ancient Sumerian legends of the gods called the Anunnaki are all about the extraterrestrial quest for gold. Beginning in 1976, author Zecharia Sitchin published his own translations of Sumerian writings in a series of books called *The Earth Chronicles*. According to Sitchin, ancient clay tablets describe the Anunnaki as an alien race who came to Earth to mine gold. He suggested that the reason we were visited in the past is that the Ancient Astronauts' home planet needed gold to keep its atmosphere stable.

Ancient gold jewelry, circa sixth century BC, Greece.
Gold has been a useful and popular currency for millennia.

Left: The gold death mask of Egyptian King Tutankhamun (King Tut).

Below: Ancient golden statue from Lima, Peru

PART TWO: THE EVIDENCE

✳

EVIDENCE FILE: INCREDIBLE ANCIENT STRUCTURES

Is there really hardcore evidence, right here on Earth, that aliens arrived in ancient times? Some say yes—and that the proof is as hard as stone.

Massive stone structures stand as mysterious monuments all over the world. To Ancient Astronaut researchers, these mega-ton monuments that have endured for centuries provide tangible evidence that, long ago, extraterrestrial visitors came to Earth. You've surely heard of some of these amazing ancient structures: the Giza pyramids in Egypt, the strange Moai heads aligned on Easter Island, Stonehenge in England. They're called megalithic because they're super large (mega-) and made of stone (-lithic). It's baffling to think that ancient people without trucks, hydraulics, or electric power moved stones like these. In today's largest construction sites and quarries, mega-machines are used to dig, cut, and lift stone. These machines use modern hydraulic technologies. Without such equipment, we couldn't build modern skyscrap-

ers. But thousands of years ago, ancient civilizations were cutting exact shapes in solid rock, transporting multiton blocks for miles, and lifting them precisely into place.

Some were built so long ago that we don't know how people were able to construct them.

We also don't know how ancient people were able to move these enormous stones. The stones used as building blocks for some of these structures are so heavy that even with modern equipment it would be a challenge. At the **Temple of Jupiter** at Baalbek in Lebanon, there are three stones estimated to weigh 800 tons—11.6 million pounds—each! A nearby quarry contains an even bigger stone monument, known as the Stone of the Pregnant Woman, which weighs 1,000 tons. To move it today would take the strength of a super crane and hydraulic trucks.

Could ancient people have possessed knowledge that was more advanced than what we have always thought? Is it possible that early

The Moai figures of Easter Island

The Temple of Jupiter, Baalbek, Lebanon

cultures were exposed to technologies beyond what we have today? Where did their tools, engineering knowledge, and stone-moving ability come from? One theory is that these unbelievable structures from the past are evidence that early humans received some extra help—make that *extraterrestrial* help.

Says Giorgio Tsoukalos:

In my opinion, the most tangible pieces of evidence that we have regarding possible extra-terrestrial technology is when we look at the ancient stonecutting techniques. In some instances, we ourselves today could not replicate what our ancestors allegedly accomplished with stonemasonry.

Could it be the ancients possessed advanced extraterrestrial technology? Around the world there are places that surely raise questions.

BUILDING ANCIENT EGYPT

The **Great Pyramid in Giza** alone may contain 2.3 million stones. Some of the stone blocks weigh 2.5 to 15 tons apiece.

Even today, scientists, archaeologists, and architects are imagining how the pyramids could have been constructed.

In the same area lies the Valley Temple, a building made out of enormous rectangular blocks. It's believed the stone blocks of Valley Temple are 100 to 200 tons each. It's hard to imagine something so heavy, but for comparison picture 40 to 80 pickup trucks piled on top of each other. Even if you can imagine how these blocks might have been cut out of limestone into perfect shapes to fit together, then you have to imagine what the workers who gazed at the gargantuan blocks of rock must have said to their bosses: "Wait, you want that moved *over where*?"

The Stone of the Pregnant Woman, Baalbek, Lebanon

How do you cut something so big? How do you move it? How do you lift it to exactly the place where it fits on the top of an intricately planned monument, especially without access to any modern technology or machinery? The ancient Egyptians didn't have cranes or modern pulleys. They had stone and copper tools. One of their technological innovations was the ramp.

How the stone was cut is a huge question all by itself. Chris Dunn, a researcher who wrote the book *Lost Technologies of Ancient Egypt*, was doing research north of Giza when he saw something interesting: a granite block with a deep, clean cut in it. It looked like a cut made by a machine, and its size perplexed him—he calculated that it must have been made by some kind of giant circular saw that would have been thirty-five feet in diameter. He also noticed large holes in the ground that were believed to be boat pits. He thought they actually might have been pits to hold these extremely large buzz saws. The saws could have been mounted in these pits, and somehow ancient people ran the stone blocks through the saws. But how would the ancient Egyptians know how to use these tools with such precision? Ancient Astronaut theorists believe they may have had input from extraterrestrials.

Some researchers wonder why ancient people would even try to do things so difficult as building the pyramids and Valley Temple. The answer may be that for them it wasn't so difficult. Ancient Astronaut theorists believe it was humans, not extraterrestrials, who built these structures with the help of ancient aliens' knowledge and tools. For example, researcher David Childress suggests that the stones could have been levitated—made weightless and moved through the air by some kind of extraterrestrial technology or device.

The Great Pyramid of Giza, in Egypt

THE MOAI HEADS OF EASTER ISLAND

In the South Pacific Ocean, 2,300 miles west of South America, giant stone figures with extra-large heads stand with their backs to the sea. The natives call them **Moai**, the silent sentinels of Easter Island. There are more than 800 of them. Some are as large as thirty-three feet high and weigh as much as eighty-two tons. The people who created the Moai were called the Rapa Nui, and historians believe their ancestors came to the island in canoes between 300 and 400 AD. The Moai statues date from 400 to 1100 AD. When the first Europeans arrived in 1722, the Rapa Nui culture was not known for having sophisticated tools and technology. Few could imagine how people with such little technological knowledge could have created the Moai statues.

Detailed image of Moai
sculptures of Easter Island

Ancient stone pillars stand tall at Göbekli Tepe, the oldest known temple on Earth

Moving the Moai into place was an even bigger riddle. Legend says that the Moai "walked" to their stone platforms. But what really happened? Modern scientists have tried and failed to duplicate the feats of the ancient Rapa Nui in moving these giant statues. In 1987, an anthropologist named Charles Love used rollers to move a nine-ton Moai replica at Western Wyoming Community College. Other researchers have tried pulling Moai with sleds. But there's a problem with the idea of moving Moai with sleds or rollers. The terrain of the area would make rollers incredibly dangerous and impossible to manipulate. This mystery remains, but Ancient Astronaut theorists believe the Rapa Nui may have communicated with otherworldly beings who provided key information and advice.

GÖBEKLI TEPE: A BURIED STONE MASTERPIECE

In 1994, on a dusty hilltop in southeastern Turkey, a Kurdish shepherd noticed the tip of a stone sticking out of his field. The next year, Klaus Schmidt, an archaeologist, began his excavation and eventually unearthed a nineteen-foot pillar. Its edges were precise, and rising from its center was a carving of a strange animal. The shepherd had stumbled upon what may be the most astonishing archaeological discovery in modern times: a very ancient human settlement known as **Göbekli Tepe**.

Test results have supported the idea that Göbekli Tepe is nearly 12,000 years old—perhaps 7,000 years older than Mesopotamia's Fertile Crescent, long heralded as the cradle of civilization. Göbekli Tepe is the oldest advanced site known on the planet. It's believed to be older than Stonehenge and the Great Pyramid in Egypt.

Stone carvings found throughout the site add to the mystery of Göbekli Tepe. The carvings depict creatures like wild boars and geese, so many animals that they suggest a story similar to the biblical story of Noah's Ark. The site happens to be less than 350 miles from Mount Ararat, the place some biblical scholars believe is the resting place of Noah's Ark. Some researchers even theorize that the events of a cataclysmic flood are recorded on the stone pillars of Göbekli Tepe.

The way Göbekli Tepe is buried suggests something else: that it was intentionally and carefully placed beneath the sand, as if it were meant to be preserved. Is it possible that Göbekli Tepe was deliberately buried in order to protect it from invaders? Or, might the intention have been to preserve it—in hopes to someday return?

THE ENDURING SECRET OF STONEHENGE

Southern England's mysterious **Stonehenge** monument, whose construction began as long ago as 3000 BC, has puzzled observers for centuries. It may have been a kind of prehistoric astronomical observatory, designed to align with the paths of the moon and the sun. It may have helped early humans keep track of eclipses and predict when the next would come. But as with all of the ancient megalithic structures around the world that have connections to activity in the heavens, there are many unanswered questions.

Stonehenge is located in Wiltshire, England, but the stones that compose it are native to southeast Wales, about 100 to 150 miles away. How did Stone Age people move the stones

such a great distance without modern technology? How did Stone Age people carefully place twenty-five-ton slabs atop thirteen-foot, fifty-ton upright stones? How did they carve all these blocks and move them here from distant rock quarries, then arrange them into a perfect outer circle that could be seen from far above ground? If the careful alignment of the stones was meant to mark the location of objects in the night sky, could much of this seemingly impossible work have been done in darkness? Were ancient people really alone in assembling Stonehenge? Might they have had otherworldly help? Was Stonehenge more than a tool to humans—perhaps a marker for extraterrestrial visitors, or even an alien landing pad?

Structures at Stonehenge in Wiltshire, England

Coral Castle, a mysterious rock structure in Homestead, Florida

A MODERN CASE FOR LEVITATING STONES?

Coral Castle in Homestead, Florida, is probably one of the most mysterious structures in North America. It's a stone garden made of sculpted blocks of ancient coral, some weighing thirty tons, spread over several acres. The intricate designs of Coral Castle's stone walls and sculptures amaze tourists. It's not an ancient site, but a structure built between 1923 and 1951. But something strange may have happened here involving an unexplained technology to move ultra heavy stones.

In 1923, a Latvian immigrant named Ed Leedskalnin began building what he originally called Rock Gate Park. Believe it or not, he insisted he wasn't using modern machinery to build it. How did he carve, move, and hoist multiton stones? Supposedly he had a tripod—a three-legged wooden apparatus. And he had chains. To move ten tons of rock? It doesn't sound like that would have worked. But he wouldn't let anybody watch him. He said that he knew the secrets of the pyramids.

42

What exactly were those secrets? All we know is what he left when he died in 1951: not just Coral Castle itself, but journals claiming that he had discovered the ancient secret of transforming stones into weightless objects. Supposedly he had reversed gravity, the way you can reverse a magnet, using it to lift stones.

Some photos taken during Coral Castle's construction show a mysterious black box that may have played a role in the work. No one ever found the box or knew what it was. And no one can explain how he built his castle either. Giorgio Tsoukalos isn't ruling out any possibilities:

The fact that one guy created these massive structures is absolutely fascinating. Am I suggesting that he did this with extraterrestrial technology? No, because I don't know. Am I excluding that possibility? No.

Coral Castle in Homestead, Florida. Could one man have moved these stones without machinery? If so, why did he keep his methods so secret?

SOUTH AMERICA'S MOUNTAIN MYSTERIES

The **Andes** are the world's longest mountain range, running 4,300 miles down the spine of South America. The mountains pass through seven countries from north to south: Venezuela, Colombia, Ecuador, Peru, Bolivia, Chile, and Argentina. Along this rugged terrain, some of the world's most incredible ancient structures can be found. Many mysteries about their origins remain.

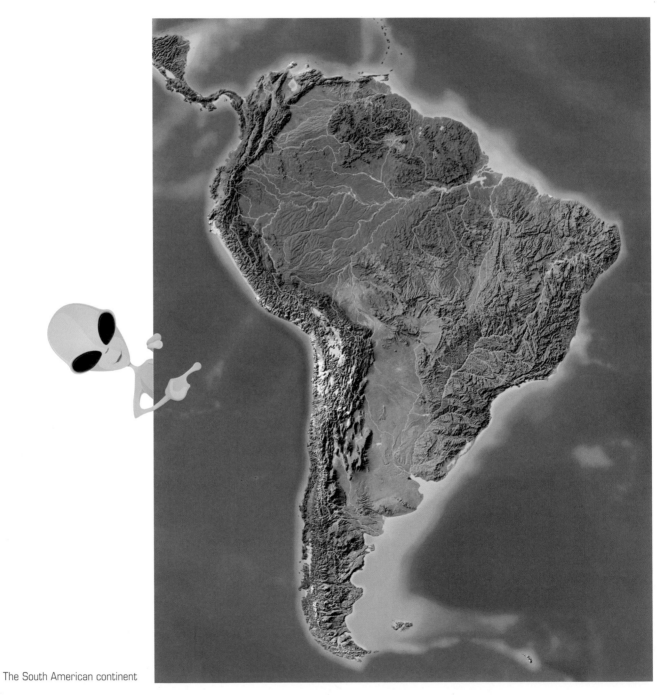

The South American continent

In Bolivia, near the border with Peru, you can find the astonishing stone temple complex called **Puma Punku**. It is isolated high in the mountains at an altitude of over 12,000 feet.

Archaeologists date the site back to approximately 200 to 1000 AD, more than 1,000 years ago, though the Austrian engineer and researcher Arthur Posnansky proposed it could be much older, as much as 15,000 years old, based on archeoastronomy, the study of how ancient people used the stars to build their cultures.

The people who lived here had neither a written language nor the wheel, yet somehow they built one of the world's most complex structures. Puma Punku contains massive blocks of red sandstone and andesite, the largest weighing 144 tons. Many are shaped like a giant letter H and arranged together almost like a set of interconnecting Lego blocks. The angles on these stones are perfect, the corners as sharp as those on modern buildings. Many of the stones have intricate designs and notches precisely chiseled into them, things like star-shaped holes, or frames, with multiple layers of depth cut into the rock like 3-D designs. The *Ancient Aliens* TV series asked stone-cutting expert Roger Hopkins about these, and he

said that today you'd need computer-controlled machines with hard, diamond-cutting tips to try to recreate them.

Some of the massive stones used to build Puma Punku supposedly were cut from quarries ten miles away, with many stones coming from sixty miles away. One theory says they were rolled to Puma Punku on logs. Is this a realistic idea? Rolling multiton stones up a mountain is questionable in itself. Once again, Ancient Aliens proponents suggest that an advanced technology involving some kind of antigravity levitation must have been used.

About a quarter mile away from Puma Punku are the ruins of Tiwanaku, built later but with what appears to be cruder construction methods. In the center of Tiwanaku is a giant andesite arch called the Gate of the Sun, cut from a single stone and weighing more than ten tons. It has been suggested that if aliens built Puma Punku, humans later built Tiwanaku and the Gate of the Sun as a place to celebrate the past visit by aliens, who were worshipped as gods.

Above: Stones like this one can weigh several tons, if not more. How did the people of ancient civilizations transport these massive objects without modern technology? Might they have had a little help from above?

Left: Do the precise and intricate details engraved on this stone indicate alien involvement or were the people of the region technologically advanced beyond their era?

Several hundred miles north of Puma Punku, in the Andes of southern Peru, one can find **Machu Picchu**, known as the Lost City of the Incas. This stunning mountaintop citadel was built around 1450 AD. Its ruins include remains of buildings, walls, and terraces. Machu Picchu isn't made of giant stones; it's made of smaller ones that have been fit together snugly. In fact, some have speculated that it has signs of molded stones. One theory holds that at Machu Picchu, small stones were transported, melted, and molded into the exact sizes needed for construction. That would require an incredible amount of heat—not your typical campfire. Not something ancient civilizations were likely to be able to produce. But maybe something that came from the stars?

The idea of melting and molding stones—rather than moving them—seems like it would have been even more useful for another incredible site in the Peruvian Andes, the ancient fortress of Sacsayhuamán in the Inca capital of Cuzco. Sacsayhuamán features astonishing stonework. The walls are put together with blocks of stone weighing as much as 300 tons, cut and shaped to lock together so tightly that, observers say, you can't even get a sheet of paper between them. And yet there is no mortar holding the walls together.

The Inca believed the site was constructed by an earlier race of people—led by a powerful god who descended from the skies. According to local legend, a bird was responsible for the seamless construction. The winged creature carried a powerful chemical in its beak—a substance capable of melting stone. Ancient Astronaut theorists suggest that this mythical "bird" may have been a spacecraft piloted by alien visitors.

An overhead shot of the elaborate and expansive stone structures of Machu Picchu

EVIDENCE FILE:
SECRETS OF THE PYRAMIDS

When you hear about pyramids, you probably think of Egypt, where the world's most famous pyramids stand. In the area of ancient Egypt are the Great Sphinx and more than 130 pyramids, built from around 2630 BC to the fourth century AD.

Really, though, there are pyramids from ancient times located all over the world. They can be found in Africa's northern Sudan and in southeast Iraq. They're in Mexico and South America. There are hundreds of pyramids in China. Many pyramids in India are like towers, straight up and tall. And there are more than 1,000 pyramids in Central America—the Mayans are thought to have built more pyramids than all other cultures in the world combined.

Pyramids in many parts of the world are extremely similar in their appearance and engineering, even though the ancient cultures that built them were separated by vast distances. People who built pyramids in Asia aren't believed to have had any contact with those who built pyramids in Central America, for example. And yet the structures are too similar not to raise any flags. The elaborate Candi Sukuh temple in Indonesia has design elements nearly identical to Mayan pyramids at Chichen Itza, which are far across the Pacific Ocean in modern-day Mexico. A Hindu temple in Cambodia mysteriously resembles a Mayan temple at Tikal. These civilizations had no known way of communicating with each other or sharing information. So how can this be?

Is it possible that civilizations spread out over five continents all built similar pyramidal structures by coincidence? Ancient Astronaut theorists believe it's no coincidence at all. They say pyramids around the globe were constructed by builders who possessed the same advanced knowledge of mathematics, astronomy, and the Earth's geophysical properties. How did they gain this shared knowledge? Says Giorgio Tsoukalos:

A possible explanation for all of this is that all of these cultures learned how to build these pyramids from the same teachers.

These teachers—you guessed it—may have been of an otherworldly origin.

The Visoko pyramids in central Bosnia and Herzegovina

LAND OF THE PHARAOHS

A good place to start any investigation of the pyramids is the Giza Plateau in Egypt. Here in the desert just outside Cairo stands the Great Pyramid, which 4,500 years ago was the tallest and most impressive man-made structure on Earth. It's 480 feet high, covers thirteen acres, and may contain 2.3 million blocks of stone. The heaviest of the stones could weigh fifteen tons. But exactly how and why the pyramid was constructed remain a mystery.

ANCIENT ALIGNMENTS WITH THE STARS

The constellation of Orion is easy to see in the winter sky in the Northern Hemisphere. Its stars, when connected by lines, form a stick figure of a man with a belt and a sword: the mighty hunter. Orion's belt points to the brightest star in the sky—Sirius.

Many cultures see Orion's belt, and the stars around it, as the heart of creation—where everything began. And structures around the world seem to be intentionally aligned in the same configuration as the stars in the belt.

Ancient Astronaut theorists believe the Mayan pyramids in Teotihuacan, Mexico, represent the stars of Orion's belt.

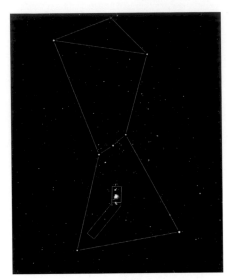

Orion's Belt, a constellation in the Milky Way Galaxy

The same arrangement is seen at the Giza pyramids in Egypt, with the belt pointing toward the city of Heliopolis, a place of worship for ancient Egyptians. Ancient Egyptians believed that performing certain ceremonies directly under Orion's belt created a sacred alignment that enabled communication with the god Osiris.

Archaeologists think the **Great Pyramid** was built around 2550 BC as the burial tomb of the Pharaoh Khufu. But some wonder if that's really the whole story. These days, we tend to mark our gravesites with just a single headstone. Using 2.3 million stones on one grave would really be overdoing it!

If the pyramids of Egypt weren't meant to be tombs, then what were they for?

The interior of the Great Pyramid has an unusual feature: four air shafts emanating from the middle of the structure—from the king's chamber and the lower queen's chamber—and exiting at different points on the pyramid's surface. Engineering expert Christopher Dunn, who has researched the pyramids, says explorers in the queen's chamber found walls coated with a layer of salt. This supported his theory that some chemistry was going on in the pyramid. Hydrochloric acid solution was being poured down one shaft, and hydrated zinc was coming down another, and when they combined in the queen's chamber they created hydrogen, a powerful energy source. He suggested that the Great Pyramid was a sort of power plant, producing energy—which may have been used by alien spacecraft.

Whether the ancient Egyptians' knowledge of the stars, and their beliefs about their gods, came from genuine contact with extraterrestrials remains one of history's most perplexing unanswered questions.

A GLOBAL PYRAMID CONSPIRACY?

Is it possible the thousands of pyramids scattered across the globe were once part of a cohesive network—one that could only be understood from the sky? Certainly, viewing the design and arrangement of many pyramids from the sky (something that none of the ancient human builders could supposedly do) offers an interesting perspective.

The Great Pyramid of Giza, with the Great Sphinx in the foreground

The **Borobudur Temple** on the Indonesian island of Java is the world's largest Buddhist monument. Built during the eighth and ninth centuries AD, this religious structure is a form of pyramid with other structures built upon it. Viewed today from above, it looks like a giant Buddhist mandala, a circular diagram that represents the cosmos and indicates a spiritual place for prayer and meditation. In short, it is a place where people could connect with the "gods." Researchers wonder why the builders would create such an intricate symbol that can only be viewed from the air.

In China, there are also giant pyramids. While flying in Shaanxi Province in China in 1947, Colonel Maurice Sheahan discovered a mysterious mound. He told the *New York Times* he believed it was a massive pyramid that seemed to dwarf the Great Pyramid of Egypt. Since then, one hundred more pyramid-shaped mounds have been identified in China, including the mausoleum of the first Qin emperor, where thousands of terracotta warrior statues were buried in the third century BC. Mainstream scientists say the mounds are simply mounds, tombs of the early emperors of China, but some researchers believe they are in fact pyramids that have been covered up and disguised as hills.

What secrets lay within these walls? Could there be a shielded historical record that could link these pyramids with visitors from another planet?

EVIDENCE FILE: BILLBOARDS FOR THE SKY GODS

All over the world, a certain type of strange landmark challenges the imagination. Someone has been drawing pictures on the surface of the Earth. Large images depict animals and humanlike figures. Giant patterns, shapes, and lines are scratched into the land by ancient people.

What's especially odd is that many of these purposefully drawn pictures on the surface of our planet are so large that they can only be seen completely from the sky, yet many of them were created before there were airplanes. Were they created by people? And who exactly, up there in the sky, is supposed to be looking at these pictures?

Ancient Astronaut theorists have ideas. The most far-out theory holds that markings visible from the sky, all over the world, could be remnants of a sort of worldwide system of airports, ancient directional signs that told extraterrestrial crafts where to land. Other theories say that ancient peoples scratched images into the Earth as greetings to visitors from the sky, or as invitations for fabled extraterrestrial visitors to return. And in the case of the intricate crop circles found in the cornfields of England and elsewhere, there has often been the feeling that aliens themselves were the artists.

THE NAZCA LINES—A PICTURE SHOW FOR THE ALIENS?

In 1927, an archaeologist hiking in Peru's Nazca desert came upon what looked like a large network of ancient roads. It turns out that the lines weren't exactly roads. Over the years, as air travel became more frequent, aerial flyovers have revealed hundreds of other designs scratched into the ground, spread over a 200-square-mile area. The lines aren't just long and straight, but are also in the shapes of spirals, triangles, trapezoids, and zig-zags. There also are giant drawings of animals, including a hummingbird, a spider, a lizard, and a humanlike figure with large eyes who has come to be called *El Astronauto*—the astronaut.

These super-sized images on the ground are known as geoglyphs, which basically means Earth pictures. Archaeologists believe they were made by the Nazca people between 500 BC and 500 AD. The desert environment in this area of Peru—with minimal rain and wind—has ensured that these mysterious images have remained intact for centuries.

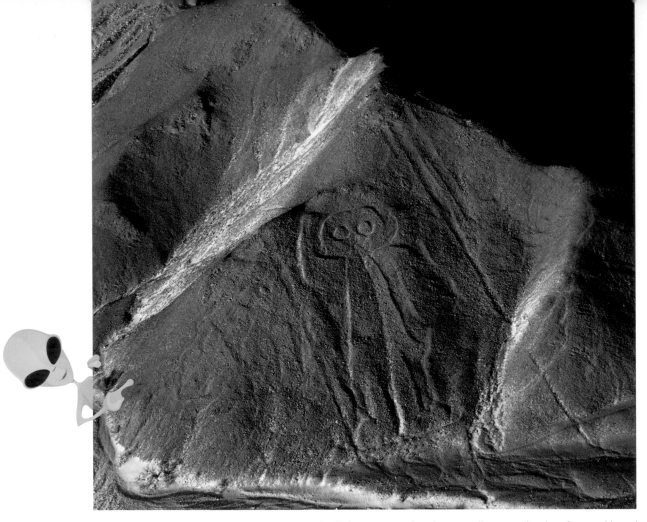

Is the *El Astronaut* carving above a rudimentary drawing of an earthbound creature or an accurate depiction of an extraterrestrial visitor?

How could the people of Nazca have created such elaborate and large designs without being able to fly overhead, and without advanced tools? Might the lines have been created with the help of otherworldly beings? Were the designs meant to be navigational markers for beings in the sky? Were they meant to commemorate an extraterrestrial encounter?

Some believe the lines are a form of communication with extraterrestrials or so-called sky gods. Nazca legends speak of star people. So these designs might be like billboards calling "Come here!" or "Land here!" The *El Astronauto* figure carved in the hills has his hand raised and seems to be waving to someone above.

Why are all these geoglyphs in this particular place? Some Ancient Aliens proponents believe the lines indicate excavations from an extensive mining operation. Nazca may have been an attractive area for spacecraft to land and an area rich in minerals that could be used as fuel. An intergalactic gas station! Perhaps the lines helped guide otherworldly visitors toward Tiwanaku and Puma Punku in Bolivia and other sites in Peru that have alien connections. Since the Nazca civilization declined about 1,500 years ago, we may never know the answer.

THE GREAT SERPENT MOUND—AN AMERICAN MYSTERY

In the early days of America's settlement, pioneers moved westward. They marveled at every kind of terrain that nature could offer: majestic and treacherous mountains, dense forests, open plains, dry deserts, wide rivers. Those pioneers needed to contend with wild animals, too.

And, every so often, they would come across a structure or piece of the landscape that clearly was not created by nature.

At the end of the 1700s, President George Washington awarded land beyond the Appalachian Mountains to Revolutionary War veterans, in 600-acre parcels, as payment for their service in battle. When the settlers arrived, they found thousands of Native American burial mounds—small hill-like bumps in the land. However, one of these mound structures was very different from the rest. The **Great Serpent Mound** in what is now Adams County, Ohio, is over 1,300 feet long. Its shape resembles an uncoiling serpent or snake. The head of the snake seems to be biting an egg. It's not randomly arranged. The head is aligned to the summer solstice sunset—the point where the sun goes down on the longest day of the year, when the Earth's Northern Hemisphere is most tilted toward the sun. The serpent's three coils point to solstice and equinox sunrises.

Overhead view of the Great Serpent Mound in Ohio

There are other mounds like this, built by ancient Native Americans. They're called effigy mounds because they're designed to depict animals or humans or gods. But the Great Serpent Mound is the largest, and, oddly, unlike most Native American mounds, it was not built for burials. It contains no human remains.

So what was it for? Or, *who* was it for?

Like the Nazca Lines in Peru, the Great Serpent Mound looks like it is meant to be viewed from the sky.

"When you see the Great Serpent Mound in Ohio, it's massively huge. And it can't really be appreciated when you're standing there looking at it. What we have here is meant to be seen from the sky," says David Childress, author of *Technology of the Gods*.

Another curious aspect of the Great Serpent Mound is where the ancient Native Americans chose to build it—on the outside edge of a five-mile wide meteor crater. The meteor strike, maybe 300 million years ago, left bizarre magnetic traces behind, possibly due to rare metals from space that the meteor contained. Testing has revealed metals, including iridium, at the site. Iridium, a rare element in the Earth's crust, has been found to be useful in the building of our own spacecraft, because it can withstand extremely high temperatures.

"If you bring a compass to the Great Serpent Mound, there're certain spots where the compass needle just keeps going," says Giorgio Tsoukalos. "So obviously we have some weird magnetic fields there."

Legend has it that birds flying over the site would fly in circles, their natural homing instincts disoriented.

Why did ancient Native Americans build a structure along a ridge where a metal like iridium, possibly from space, was concentrated and available? Ancient Astronaut theorists believe extraterrestrials may have come to this site to mine iridium for their spacecrafts. They note numerous caves found in the crater swell beneath the mound as evidence. Might this explain why the Great Serpent Mound was built on a scale that made it visible from the sky?

THE CARNAC STONES: ANCIENT INTERGALACTIC SPACE STATION?

On the northwest coastline of France is a town named Carnac, where one can find the remnants of a truly remarkable ancient site. The **Carnac Stones** are a collection of more than 3,000 massive rocks, arranged in rows and other shapes, and spreading across more than

two miles of French countryside. The prehistoric arrangement of rocks is believed to have been put together eons ago, as far back as 4000 BC. It's the largest collection of megalithic standing stones in the world. Like the Nazca Lines, it can be seen from high in the sky.

Mythology says the stones originally represented invading Roman soldiers, turned to stone by Merlin the Magician. It's a nice story. But no one knows exactly why ancient people decided to arrange the massive stones in such a way.

There is a theory that the stones were cut and positioned in a way that created some sort of geomagnetic field, which might have been used to guide alien airships, like an airport beacon or GPS system. According to a concept known as the World Grid Theory, certain places on our planet contain higher magnetic forces than others. Some Ancient Astronauts theorists believe that many of the megalithic structures around Earth—from the pyramids in Egypt to Machu Picchu in Peru—are located at specific points that could be harnessing an ancient world energy grid. The idea is that extraterrestrial spacecraft traveling extraordinary distances would need energy from our planet, and would need to know where to get it.

There are also clues indicating that early people may have used the Carnac Stones, like Stonehenge in England, as a primitive calendar. At one end of the Carnac alignment, aerial researchers identified a stone circle, similar to the one at Stonehenge. At the other end, investigators on the ground discovered a rectangle of stones that had been buried for centuries.

Both groupings appeared precisely placed to predict the summer and the winter solstice. And when examined even more closely from above, the solstice points and the alignment of Carnac's many rows of stones reveal yet another geometric phenomenon covering many square miles: the shape of a Pythagorean, or right, triangle. How could the builders of Carnac have had knowledge of a sophisticated mathematical theorem—millenia before its discovery by the Greek mathematician Pythagoras?

PYTHAGORAS: LORD OF THE TRIANGLES

Pythagoras was an ancient Greek philosopher, mathematician, and religious leader, born around 570 BC. He is credited with developing a mathematical description of a right triangle that we still use today, more than 2,500 years later. The formula can be used to calculate real-life areas and distances. The Pythagorean theorem states that in any triangle with a right angle (90 degrees), there is a fixed relation-

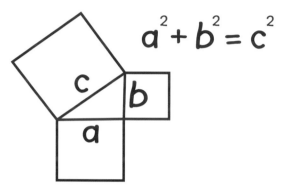

Pythagorean theorem

ship between the length of the hypotenuse (the side opposite the right angle) and the two other sides. If the hypotenuse line is called c, and the other two sides a and b, then $a^2 + b^2 = c^2$. So if you know the length of any two sides of the triangle, you can calculate the length of the third. The same formula means that the areas of squares drawn from each side would also have this mathematical relationship. In this illustration, for example, the area of box a plus the area of box b equals the area of box c.

Regarding the Carnac Stones, Ancient Aliens expert Giorgio Tsoukalos wonders:

We're talking Stone Age time, and they knew about A squared plus B squared equals C squared? They knew about it, yes, but why? Who told them this? At the time, extraterrestrials told our ancestors, put this stone here, put this stone there, with the idea that a future generation would have to stumble across this mathematical riddle, that somebody would say, "hold on a second!" This was erected during the Stone Age, yet here we have advanced mathematics. How is this possible?

CROP CIRCLES: HOAX . . . OR OTHERWORLDLY MESSAGES?

Crop circles are elaborate designs and pictures that have been cut into the crops in vast fields of corn, wheat or other kinds of crops. Stalks of corn, for example, are flattened within a field to create lines and designs. They tend to follow geometric patterns or resemble ancient symbols. They can be really beautiful. Most important, they are truly appreciated only when viewed from the sky.

We know crop circles not as an ancient phenomenon but as a modern one. Any patterns that might have been made in crops thousands of years ago would be gone by now, of course, so it's impossible to know how far back this practice really began. The 2002 movie *Signs* shows just how frightening crop circles can be. In the film, a Pennsylvania farm family notices crop circles in their cornfield. At first, conferring with local police, they figure that it's just a prank by local kids. Not long afterward, though, the farmer is shocked to glimpse a leathery, gray alien in his cornfield. Eventually, alien spacecraft begin a hostile attack on Earth. The crop circles were a sort of warning from the aliens.

In real life, reports of crop circles go back for hundreds of years. In the early years, patterns found in fields might have been attributed to a mythical "mowing devil." But especially since the 1970s, a lot of strange reports have "cropped" up in the news. Almost all of these discoveries have been in England, some of them near the mysterious Stonehenge site. Over the years, crop circle designs came to be associated with UFOs and UFO sightings. A theory emerged that extraterrestrials were making these designs as a way to establish contact with our modern civilization.

Then, in 1991, two British pranksters, Doug Bower and Dave Chorley, came forward and confessed that they were the ones responsible for many of the crop circles. They showed how they could make crop circles overnight, in darkness, using simple tools. After that, for many people the issue of crop circles was over—dismissed forever as nothing but a hoax. But some researchers remain skeptical that a single pair of middle-aged men could have created hundreds of designs in the dead of night with little more than a few wood boards and some rope.

During the years that followed Bower and Chorley's confession, crop circles continued to appear in the English countryside and around the world. Some were surely the work of artists or jokesters. But after studying soil samples and grain dispersion patterns in the disturbed

Crop circle in a field near Oxfordshire, England

farmland, researchers have concluded that it would be impossible for all of these designs to be man-made. In 1991, biophysicist Dr. William Levengood offered a new theory. After spending ten years studying crop circle sites and samples, he concluded that they were created by a complex energy system that he called a spinning plasma vortex, which comes down from somewhere high up in the atmosphere.

For some, crop circles and their possible connection to otherworldly life remain an unsolved mystery. Are they purely man-made hoaxes? Or are they evidence of something powerful from above?

EVIDENCE FILE:
DID ANCIENT ANCESTORS
HAVE AIRPLANES?

On December 17, 1903, in Kitty Hawk, North Carolina, brothers Orville and Wilbur Wright made history and changed the world. In the airplane they built, they showed it was possible for a man-made object heavier than air to fly like the birds and the bees. It was a remarkable break-through and one of humanity's greatest innovations. Large hot-air balloons had floated people into the air in big baskets decades before, and there had been experiments with gliders, but it wasn't until the start of the twentieth century that people mastered the power of controlled flight.

Or was it? Ancient relics and writings could show that long-ago civilizations knew what airplanes or even spaceships looked like—and maybe even tried them out.

Is it a bird? Or a plane?

The Pyramid of Djoser is one of the many marvels in the great necropolis (an ancient cemetery) in Saqqara, Egypt, which is nicknamed City of the Dead. Dating back more than 4,000 years, Djoser is the oldest of Egypt's ninety-seven pyramids. It's sometimes called the Step Pyramid because it looks like a staircase.

It was around this pyramid in 1898 that French archaeologists unearthed an ancient tomb containing the burial remains of Pa-di-Imen, an official from the third century BC. Among the buried items they discovered was a small, wooden model of what looked like a bird, near a papyrus bearing the inscription: "I want to fly." The artifact was sent to the Cairo Museum in Egypt and was kept alongside other ancient bird figurines. But in 1969, Egyptologist Dr. Khalil Messiha was examining the bird collection and noticed something really different about the Saqqara bird and its wings.

They don't look like the flapping kind of wings that a bird has. They look like the straight, fixed wings that a plane has. The relic looks like a toy airplane.

If you've ever visited the Smithsonian

Saqqara bird figurine, Saqqara, Egypt

National Air and Space Museum in Washington, D.C., you've probably had a chance to learn about aeronautics concepts like lift and drag, which are fundamental to how an airplane can defy gravity. A lot of it has to do with the shape of the wings, curved in a way to create lift, designed aerodynamically with rounded edges to minimize wind drag, and with added design features to stabilize a plane in flight.

In the Saqqara bird, experts saw a strangely aerodynamic design, with wings rounded and thicker in some places to provide lift. And on the back there is what looks like a rudder, something that the tail of a plane has but that the tail of a bird doesn't need. Could this be a model of a plane? People knew what birds looked like back then and made detailed images of them. This was different. Could the ancient Egyptians have possessed the power of flight?

In 2006, aviation and aerodynamics expert Simon Sanderson built a scale model of the Saqqara bird, five times larger than the original, to check out the idea. He ran tests exposing it to wind and found that it produced lift—it could have flown! Computer models seemed to confirm that the Saqqara bird is airworthy. It actually seems like a highly developed glider, with a design similar to what is used today.

How did such an aircraft get its power to fly? A glider usually is launched in some way. Modern methods usually use a tow plane that pulls the glider into the air using cords, then releases it. How might the ancient Egyptians have launched the Saqqara bird? Well, they could have used a catapult. Some glider enthusiasts today use a bungee cord system to shoot themselves into the air.

But if the Saqqara bird model is capable of flight, where would ancient Egyptians have acquired such technology? German astronautical engineer Algund Eenboom says, "I think that people in ancient times were visited by beings coming not from this Earth, and they gave us culture and scientific technologies to improve our life on Earth."

ANOTHER PREHISTORIC PLANE?

Far across the globe, seven thousand miles from Egypt, another ancient figurine looks even more like some kind of an aircraft—and passes flight tests with flying colors.

The dense jungles and rugged mountains of Columbia contain a vast number of archaeological sites. Some treasure hunters believe El Dorado, the legendary city of gold, even lies hidden here. While that mythical metropolis has never been found, early in the twentieth century, tomb robbers searching along the Magdalena River stumbled upon a gravesite dating back to a civilization known as the Quimbaya, from perhaps 1,500–2,000 years ago, a time referred to as pre-Columbian in the Western Hemisphere because it was before Europeans like Christopher Columbus arrived in this "new world."

Among the objects found there were hundreds of small, two- to three-inch gold figurines. "Many of those looked like insects and fish. However, out of those hundreds that they found, they also found about a dozen that are eerily reminiscent of modern-day fighter jets," Giorgio Tsoukalos says. "They have a triangular shape. They have an upright tail fin, stabilizers, and a fuselage. And they have nothing in common with anything similar in nature."

There's not a bird or a bug on Earth that looks quite like the "gold flyer" figurine.

"There is not a single insect in the world which has got its wings at the bottom," said Philip Coppens, the Belgian author and Ancient Astronaut theorist. "Now when you exclude the possibility that it's an insect, one of the things which remain is the fact that this is actually, yes, what it looks like: a plane."

In fact, it looks a little like a space shuttle. Could these gold objects really be proof that Earth has been visited by ancient aliens?

It was time for some more testing. In 1997, German aviation experts, including Algund Eenboom and Peter Belting, built a scale-model replica of the Goldflyer, fully equipped with landing gear and a working engine. They wanted to see if it could really get into the air and fly. It looked like it could. Eenboom said they didn't need to change the design because "the shape was perfect. Everything was already done by the native people 2,000 years ago."

Replica of the gold flyer figurine from the Quimbaya civilization

The remote-controlled flyer took off down a runway . . . and flew!

Two examples from opposite sides of the planet. Two aerodynamically sound models of flying objects, eons before the Wright brothers perfected the airplane and took off into the North Carolina sky. Were they just interesting designs dreamed up by our ancient ancestors? Lucky guesses? Artistic representations of birds or bugs? Or were they based on something people saw that wasn't found in nature?

THOSE MAGNIFICENT GODS IN THEIR FLYING MACHINES

Within some of the world's most ancient texts, a number of them religious in nature, are descriptions that sound like flying machines coming down from the heavens. One of the most referenced stories of ancient aircraft is found in a surprising place, the Bible. In the Book of Ezekiel, the prophet describes a flying chariot containing wheels within wheels and powered by angels. The biblical text's description of something coming from the sky and landing and beings emerging from it is quite explicit:

> Then I looked, and behold, a whirlwind was coming out of the north, a great cloud with raging fire engulfing itself; and brightness was all around it and radiating out of its midst like the color of amber, out of the midst of the fire. Also from within it came the likeness of four living creatures. And this was their appearance: they had the likeness of a man . . . Each one had four faces, and each one had four wings. Their legs were straight, and the soles of their feet were like the soles of calves' feet. They sparkled like the color of burnished bronze. The hands of a man were under their wings on their four sides; and each of the four had faces and wings.

The prophet said this was the appearance of the Lord. Traveling in what sounds like a spaceship?

Elsewhere, other ancient mythologies include tales of strange flying craft. Legends of air travel are found in ancient Africa and the Middle East. According to the Kebra Nagast, a holy book of the Ethiopians written sometime in the sixth century AD, the Queen of Sheba was given a gift of a flying carpet by King Solomon of Israel. The Kebra Nagast also describes how King Solomon used his flying airship to make maps of the world.

India is considered one of the oldest civilizations, with settlements dating back more than 11,000 years. It is also home to several of the oldest records of ancient technologies. Ancient Sanskrit texts dating as far back as 1500 BC refer to flying machines called vimanas.

A text known as the Vymaanika Shaastra gets into some details about how vimanas may have flown. The Vymaanika Shaastra is not proven to be an ancient text. It was "revealed" in 1952 with authorship attributed to an Indian mystic who claimed that the text was psychically delivered to him. But the early descriptions of vimanas truly are from ancient times.

Although mainstream historians believe the vimana texts are purely myths, many of the documents contain passages that seem to describe modern machinery and technology. And it's important to remember that myths come from somewhere, often from events witnessed by people who invent stories to explain what they don't completely understand.

EVIDENCE FILE: UNDERWATER WORLDS AND LOST LANDS

Oceans cover more than 70 percent of Earth, and more than 95 percent of the world beneath the seas remains unexplored. What lies below the surface of our own planet remains as much a mystery as the edges of outer space. That means clues to our civilization's past await us at our shores. Is there evidence down below that something from far above has paid Earth a visit?

Earth, as seen from space

An example of what a sunken city, like Atlantis, might look like

Historians know that much of the landscape sunk within the deep today was once on perfectly dry land, before floods and other events submerged it. The last ice age lasted perhaps 100,000 years and ended about 10,000 years ago. Warming caused ice to melt, turned it into water in volumes high enough to raise sea levels, and the water overflowed once-inhabited lands. Researcher Graham Hancock says 10 million square miles of land—roughly the size of Europe and China together—was flooded around the world during the meltdown, and what was on those lands was erased from history, "just rubbed from the record."

"All over the world there are sunken cities," says author David Childress. "There's more than 200 known sunken cities in the Mediterranean alone."

The idea that ancient cities got flooded and submerged isn't so crazy. But something doesn't add up. Using advanced technologies for exploring beneath the ocean's surface, researchers are finding underwater complexes and sophisticated monuments around the world that defy historical records. Some areas where sophisticated structures lie underwater are calculated by scientists to have been flooded many thousands of years ago, possibly before primitive human civilizations had technology advanced enough to create them. So, then, who built these ancient underwater mysteries?

THE SEARCH FOR ATLANTIS

A giant, lost island called Atlantis, home to a thriving civilization, is believed by some to have sat in the Atlantic Ocean (as its name suggests). Most of our information about it comes from the ancient Greek philosopher Plato who, in 360 BC, wrote two books of dialogues telling stories of the past. Plato described Atlantis as an advanced, war-making city, ringed by circular walls that flourished 9,000 years before his time. There are descriptions of huge palaces for kings. Atlantis had huge naval forces, which it used to conquer other parts of the world. As the story goes, after a failed attempt to invade Athens, disaster struck in the form of cataclysmic destruction that sank the entire island.

A city like this that thrived before the earliest civilizations are believed to have formed would be truly remarkable. It would be evidence of a culture that was somehow far more advanced than Stone Age people could have been. But is there any proof that Atlantis existed? People have been looking.

According to Plato, Atlantis was located beyond the Pillars of Hercules, which would be near modern Gibraltar, off the coast of Spain. But in 1968, archaeologist J. Manson Valentine believed he found part of Atlantis when he discovered an unusual rock formation off the coast of North Bimini Island—amid the Bahama islands near Florida. Along with fellow archaeologists Jacques Mayol, Robert Angore, and Harold Climo, Valentine found beach rock piled atop other beach rock, with stones wedged in between in a way that nature never could have arranged. It seemed to be a remnant of an ancient city. Atlantis?

Simulation of what Zelitsky found of the coast of Cuba

In the year 2000, while mapping the seafloor off the western coast of Cuba, a Russian expedition led by oceanographer Paulina Zelitsky spotted unnatural stone structures deep below the water there. The structures were more than a half mile down, too far for divers to explore. Instead the expedition sent down equipment, including cameras and sonar, that could create images of the seafloor and underwater objects. The images they retrieved showed rectangular shapes and very large structures that seemed to have wide avenues. Thirty geometric structures emerged, appearing to be the remains of streets, buildings, tunnels, and pyramids—all at a depth of 2,200 feet below the surface. It looked like a man-made city. Strangely, the Bahaman ruins lie on the edge of the Bermuda Triangle, an area of ocean covering more than 500,000 square miles that's known for magnetic anomalies, UFO sightings, and unexplained disappearances of aircraft and ships.

ISLANDS FROM THE SKY?

Even as researchers comb the oceans in search of evidence of Atlantis, another theory has been considered. Greek mythology contains stories of so-called gods and goddesses that fell from the sky—and became islands. Were these stories completely made up? Did anything really come down from the sky to inspire them? The stories give some Ancient Astronaut theorists like Giorgio Tsoukalos an idea:

> In ancient Greece, we have a number of myths which describe islands—bronze gleaming islands that fell from the sky and landed in water. I don't think that Atlantis therefore was an actual stationary, physical island. Atlantis, according to Plato, disappeared in one night. See, I don't think that Atlantis sank, I think Atlantis lifted off.

A BURIED UNDERGROUND HAVEN: REFUGE FROM SKY WARS?

The region of central Turkey called Cappadocia is known for its ancient stone dwellings, but newer homes have been built in towns there. In 1963, in the town of Derinkuyu, workers renovating a home made an extraordinary discovery. A cave wall was opened, revealing a passageway to an underground city thousands of years old and more than 280 feet deep.

The city seems to have been constructed underground on purpose, rather than buried by disaster or the sands of time. Many ventilation shafts brought air down. There was space for perhaps 20,000 people, as well as livestock. Why was it built? And how? Some experts find it perplexing that an ancient civilization could have built such an elaborate underground refuge without help from another civilization.

Some archaeologists and scholars think Derinkuyu was meant to be a temporary shelter from invasion, built around 800 BC by the Phrygians, a Bronze Age people allied with the Trojans. Others believe it was built by the Hittites, a warrior people mentioned in the Bible who flourished hundreds of years earlier.

But Ancient Aliens researchers believe this underground complex could be a shelter against aerial bombardment—from an ancient time when no airplanes existed. Sacred Zoroastrian texts tell of the sky god Ahura Mazda instructing a human prophet to build a kind of underground refuge. Ahura Mazda was said to soar through the sky in a divine chariot, waging war against his eternal enemy, Angra Mainyu, the demon of destruction. Did the ancient people of Derinkuyu really go underground to avoid becoming casualties in an extraterrestrial battle between sky gods?

Could Atlantis, then, have been a landing area for ancient aliens, before the end of Earth's last ice age? And could there be other alien cities submerged underwater?

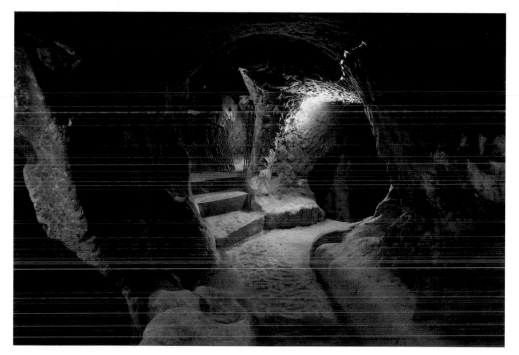

A cave city in Derinkuyu, Turkey

YONAGUNI, JAPAN

Yonaguni is the westernmost inhabited island of Japan in the Pacific Ocean. Historians believe the first inhabitants arrived there during prehistoric times. The island today is known for producing a potent variety of rice wine enjoyed by locals, and for the large number of hammerhead sharks that swim off its beaches. The sharks aren't the only fascinating thing lurking in the nearby sea.

In 1987, divers made a shocking discovery near the Yonaguni coast. A massive complex of

Underwater ruins at Yonaguni, Japan

stone formations lay hidden a mere sixty feet beneath the ocean's surface. One structure resembled a massive stepped pyramid, the size of two football fields. There were passageways and stairways. There were tools and engravings that clearly weren't created randomly by nature. Experts call it one of the greatest discoveries in the history of underwater archaeology.

"There is a stone in which is carved a face almost twenty-three feet tall," says Japanese professor Masaaki Kimura. "Our first impression was that it looked a lot like the Moai on Easter Island, then we began to realize that it strongly resembled the Sphinx, which guarded the pyramids, and we wondered if that might be the function the face is also serving here."

Geological evidence suggests that the structures were created before being covered by water during the meltdown of the last ice age. If the Yonaguni complex was built when ocean levels were lower—maybe 14,000 years ago—it was done so when humans were still dwelling in caves as hunters and gatherers. Which raises a question: how could those hunter-gatherers possibly have built such elaborate structures?

Did they have help from somewhere?

"The engineering is just beyond the capacity of Stone Age civilizations," says UFO researcher Bill Birnes.

One other bizarre feature of the Yonaguni complex is that it lies in an area long suspected of having some kind of extraterrestrial activity—a zone called the Dragon's Triangle. As with the Bermuda Triangle, it's an area that planes and ships avoid traveling through. Both areas have been associated with strange magnetic interference.

And, coincidentally, the Earth's twenty-fifth parallel north, which rings the globe 25 degrees above the equator, cuts through both the Bermuda Triangle and the Dragon's Triangle—which would be convenient for aliens using both areas as landing bases.

LEGENDARY CITIES OF ANCIENT INDIA

In 2001, researchers from India's Oceanic Institute were assigned to investigate water pollution in the Gulf of Khambhat, an inlet of the Arabian Sea on the west coast of India. Seven miles from shore, they found more than they had been looking for. Sonar images revealed a huge network of stone buildings and structures.

"They look like cities that have been submerged for a very long time at a time when mainstream archaeology tells us there were no cities anywhere in the world," says researcher Graham Hancock. Divers retrieved artifacts including wood and pottery shards—some believed to be as much as 32,000 years old. There are experts who say large-scale Indian civilization only goes back 4,000 or 5,000 years, though Hindu scholars say their civilization dates back much further. Do the findings in the Gulf of Khambhat prove them right?

Farther north off India's coast, another discovery was made under the sea. Divers found the remains of what might be the ancient holy city of Dwarka, said to be the dwelling place of Lord Krishna, a deity worshipped across many traditions of Hinduism. Hindu texts explain that a ruler of the kingdom of Salwa attacked Lord Krishna in Dwarka in a fiery sky battle. Ancient Astronaut theorists believe the descriptions of the battle suggest the use of alien technology and even spacecraft.

According to the ancient texts, a spacecraft attacked Dwarka, raining down energy weapons that resembled lightning. It destroyed large parts of the city in this way. When this happened, Krishna responded by firing weapons at the spacecraft—arrows that roared like thunder and resembled bolts of lightning. The legend says Krishna eventually left Earth, and the ocean consumed his city.

It all seems like pure mythology—but the offshore discovery made some people reconsider. How much of the Dwarka story was real? Did India's ancestors witness a war between flying gods? Or were these celestial figures really extraterrestrial beings?

COULD THE EARTH BE HOLLOW?

Conventional geology says that below Earth's surface is a rocky crust up to thirty miles thick. Below that is molten rock, heated by the planet's core, with a solid center of iron and nickel the size of the moon. It's all too deep for scientists to have examined firsthand. Some very speculative theorists suggest that maybe things are different inside our planet. Maybe the Earth is hollow, and possibly a dwelling place for advanced civilizations from other worlds.

The idea that the Earth might be hollow dates back to the astronomer **Edmund Halley**, who is best known for his breakthrough in accurately predicting the cycle of Halley's Comet. In 1691, he suggested that Earth was hollow with several spheres inside. Ideas like this didn't go away. In 1818, former U.S. Army Captain John Cleves Symmes, Jr., announced that there were vast openings at each pole, where we could enter "Inner Earth." In 1864, Jules Verne revived ideas of a hollow planet with his fantastical science-fiction novel *A Journey to the Center of the Earth*.

Edmund Halley

The most controversial claim by Hollow Earth proponents is that the famous Arctic explorer Admiral Richard E. Byrd actually flew a plane near the North Pole into the interior of the Earth in 1947. If he did, he didn't tell anyone about it publicly. It is described in his supposed "secret diary," which was published in the 1990s, long after his death. Skeptics claim the diary is a forgery and not really written by Byrd.

THE MYSTERY OF LAKE TITICACA

The highest body of water in the world navigable by ships is **Lake Titicaca**, nested in the Andes Mountains of Peru at an elevation of 12,500 feet. It's huge—118 miles long and 50 miles wide. It's the largest lake in all of South America, if you take into account the amount of water it holds. For centuries, local legends have spoken of a lost underwater city called Wanaku.

In August of 2000, an Italian team of divers and archaeologists launched an underwater investigation of the legendary lake. There, submerged under one hundred feet of water, the team uncovered traces of a paved road, a stone terrace, and a wall nearly a half mile long. They also found a large, sculptured stone head that resembled sculptures at the nearby ancient city of Tiwanaku, long thought by Ancient Astronaut theorists to have extraterrestrial origins.

Local legends suggested that giants had come long ago to create the city of Tiwanaku and that the lake is where the world began. Elder indigenous people spoke of an underwater city and lights from above connecting with the lake. Could the ruins found beneath Lake Titicaca be the remains of the ancient city of Wanaku? Could it really have been another of the ancient underwater cities possibly built with the help of alien visitors?

Lake Titicaca in Peru

THE GARDEN OF EDEN

Everyone knows about Adam and Eve from the Book of Genesis in the Bible. The Old Testament says they were humanity's first people, created by God and placed in the Garden of Eden, thereby beginning the human race. **Was there really a Garden of Eden? If so, where was it?**

Genesis is very specific about where. "A river flows out of Eden to water the garden, and from there it divides and becomes four branches," the biblical text says. It names two rivers that exist today, the Tigris and Euphrates, and two that no longer exist, Pishon and Gihon. The location is modern day Iraq, and the inlet of water is known as the Persian Gulf. Researchers believe the third river, now known as the Karun River, runs through Iran and joins the Euphrates just north of the Persian Gulf. In 2010, satellite imagery revealed a separate dry riverbed that once flowed through northern Arabia and also joined with the Euphrates. These four rivers could have combined at the present day Persian Gulf into one river that flowed through the Garden of Eden.

The large gulf isn't a river, of course, but it may once have been land with a river running through it. It's believed that as polar ice caps melted following the last ice age, the waters of what is now the Indian Ocean flooded the land and formed the Persian Gulf. Remember—the biblical book of Genesis also tells of a monumental flood, in the story of Noah's Ark. Science and the Bible seem to tell the same story different ways.

But the Bible isn't the only set of stories centered on this region that is said to be the birthplace of humanity. The area of those rivers in the ancient world was known as Mesopotamia. It was home to the first civilization, the Sumerians. Linguistic research indicates Sumerians used the word "eden" to mean a plain, which might describe a fertile garden like Eden. And Sumerian mythology includes references to an otherwordly race named the Anunnaki who came to Earth and created the first modern human beings.

THE COSMIC ENERGIES
OF CRYSTAL SKULLS

Crystals are associated with supernatural powers and mystical energy in cultures around the world. Sparkling crystals found in nature are believed by many to have healing powers. Man-made crystal balls have been employed by seers trying to connect with spirits and peer into the future. And then there are crystal skulls—reportedly found in ancient locations around the world, fully formed and resembling human heads. Could the crystal skulls have mystical properties—and might they in fact have extraterrestrial origins? Ancient Aliens proponists think so.

In 1924, British explorer Frederick Albert Mitchell-Hedges, a colorful adventurer who often spoke of discovering lost cities, was in the jungle of Belize in Central America. He and his daughter, Anna, were with an expedition party exploring the ruins of Lubantuun, an ancient Mayan city that dates back to the eighth century AD.

As the story goes, Anna climbed to the top of a crumbling pyramid hoping to see the ocean. The sun shone down through a crack in the structure and hit something that seemed to light up. It turned out to be a crystal skull, weighing eleven pounds seven ounces. Apart from a detached jaw piece found nearby, it appeared to be carved from a single piece of rock crystal. According to Mitchell-Hedges' story, when the natives saw it, it was like their god had returned. The explorer presented the crystal skull to the high priest, and they celebrated and worshipped it.

Mayan elders believed that, in ancient times, thirteen crystal skulls were buried in secret places around the world. Legend says that when the thirteen skulls come together, something significant will change in the world. Many crystal skulls have since emerged. Some obviously are man-made modern versions and not ancient—and we don't have all thirteen yet. A crystal skull given the name Synergy reportedly was retrieved from the Andes Mountains. When a man from a tribe in Micronesia saw the photo of Synergy, he thought it was his ancestor. In this region, ancestral myths talk of people descending from the sky and later returning from the

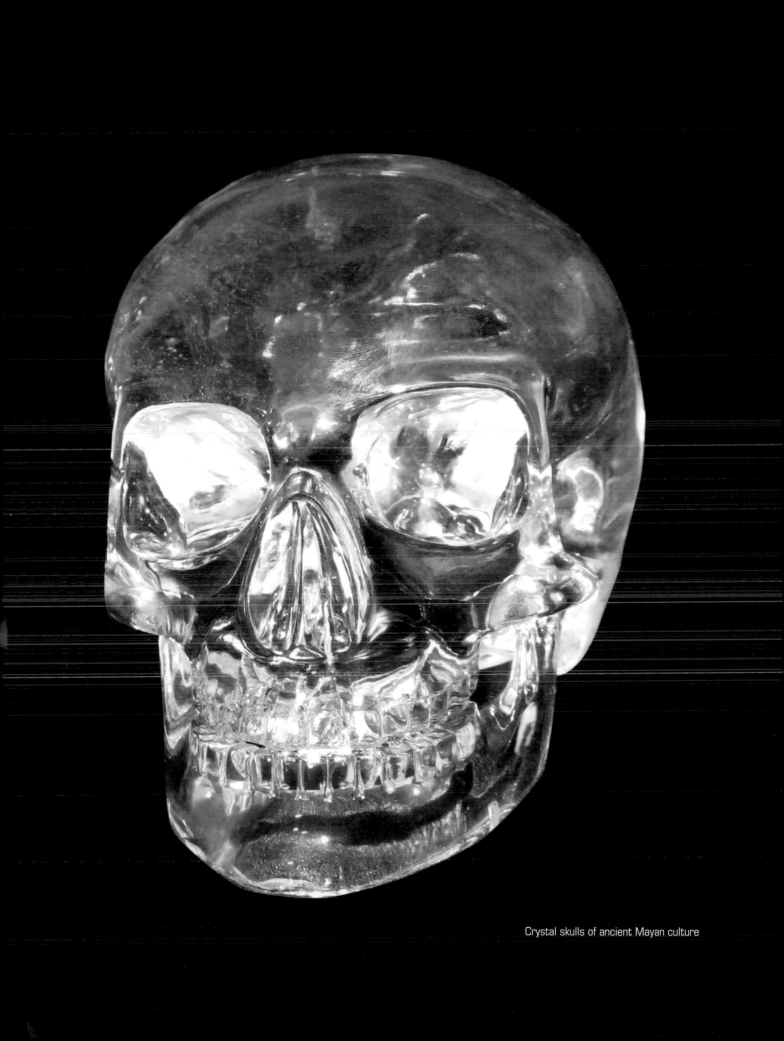

Crystal skulls of ancient Mayan culture

Some believe that crystal skulls are so perfectly formed that they cannot have been man-made and may be part of mythologies that link ancient events to otherworldly visits. Ancient Astronaut theorists note that **quartz crystal** has high-tech properties—it has been used in modern science in everything from radios to computer displays.

Like computer disks, crystals can also store information. Some Ancient Alien theorists speculate that a crystal skull could hold much more data than any computer device we have now. When multiple crystal skulls are brought together, perhaps to interface with one another, could it bring mankind untold knowledge from the stars?

ALIENS AND DEADLY WEAPONS

Fire that burns underwater. Fighter planes that don't need pilots. Rockets capable of destroying entire cities. Ancient history is filled with accounts of incredibly powerful weapons strangely similar to those in use today. Ancient lore even describes a weapon close to something we have seen only in the movies: light sabers! What were ancient authors really describing?

Throughout history, people have developed ever more deadly weapons: from rocks to spears, from swords to gunpowder, guns, bombs, and missiles. Much of our advance in deadly weaponry came from the ability to harness fire. Fire was powerful itself. It gave us the abillity to shape metal into swords, create explosions, and make other implements of destruction. Did the first secrets of fire, metalworking, and explosives come purely from humanity's own ingenuity? Or could extraterrestrials have helped us along with these powers—perhaps to help us defend ourselves, to advance our civilization? Perhaps to help us become more like them? Ancient tales involving fire, weapons, and not-of-this-world beings leave a lot of unanswered questions.

THE DAWN OF FIRE

Fire occurs naturally on Earth, but in one culture after another around the globe, fire is described as an element given to people by "the gods"—or stolen from them. Native American traditions often describe fire as stolen from the world above. Maori legends from New Zealand describe the theft of fire from the gods. In Greek legends, too—they have Prometheus stealing fire from the gods. Ancient Astronaut theorists say the fact that there are such similar myths around the world could be evidence that it was extraterrestrial beings, perhaps believed to be gods, who delivered firepower and knowledge of fire to humans.

ANCIENT SWORDS OF STEEL AND MAGIC

According to archaeologists, metal weaponry was made in the Bronze Age, beginning around 3300 BC. One major advance was steel, made with iron and carbon and forged with fire. Steel could be made thin and stay strong, so it became an ideal material for swords. But while the forging of iron isn't very complicated, the creation of steel is a more complex scientific process. Who or what was responsible for this innovation?

Ancient tales speak of magic swords crafted from steel, as if it took a wizard—or maybe a being even more extraordinary—to craft one. Villages might have one or two steel swords, and warlords sought to find all the steel swords and take them for their armies. In some cultures, people didn't look village blacksmiths who worked with metal in the eye because blacksmiths were thought to have evil power.

The idea that metalworking was a dark and magical process was so prevalent in the ancient world that in Greek mythology, even mega-god Zeus looked upon his son Hephaestus, the god of metallurgy, with suspicion. Hephaestus made armor for the gods. Zeus was so suspicious of Hephaestus that he flung him from the heavens, where he landed on the island of Lemnos. That was all just mythology—supposedly. But there is a real city called Hephaestia, named after him. And according to some ancient stories, Hephaestus actually lived among the people of Lemnos. Could he have actually been present in ancient Greece? And if so, might he have been not a god, but an ancient alien visitor?

Swords have been thought to have magical properties throughout history. This is a monument of swords commemorating King Harold Fairhair (850–933 AD) who was responsible for unifying Norway.

JAPAN'S SWORD INNOVATIONS

Stories of metal weaponry and its otherworldly orgin are not limited to ancient Greece. Japanese legend says that in 700 AD, the swordsmith Amakuni and his son Amakura sealed themselves away in their blacksmith shop in an effort to forge the perfect weapon. For seven days and seven nights, they prayed to the Shinto gods to guide them. They emerged from their isolation with a curved, single-edged sword resembling no blade ever made before. At that time, the swords were double-edged, heavy, and prone to breakage. Swordsmiths thought Amakuni's curved sword was ridiculous. But when the emperor returned from battle with an army equipped with those curved swords, Amakuni counted the blades. There were dozens—hundreds, even—and none were broken.

Replica of an ancient Japanese sword

What was the secret behind Amakuni's radical sword design, one that deviated from what had been used for more than a thousand years? Was he simply ahead of his time? Or could he really have received otherworldly guidance during the seven days and nights he and his son prayed to the Shinto gods?

The history of the Japanese sword is a long one, and it includes mythological beliefs that the sun goddess Amaterasu gave her great-great grandson a sword when she sent him down to rule over the earth. According to the beliefs of the Samurai, higher beings called Kami began human life. And in order for humans to experience the divine nature of Kami, they had to undergo purification rituals, which were performed when making a new blade. Swordsmiths chanted when hammering new blades as if hammering their chants into the metal. Could Amakuni and Amakura have come in contact with Kami? Might alien beings have chosen Amakuni, the greatest sword maker of his time, to hold the knowledge of this new technology?

Maybe the best-known Japanese swords are those of the Samurai, ultrasharp precision instruments whose quality is difficult to produce even today. In Shingon Buddhism, the sword has a life of its own. It's not that the Samurai selects the blade—the blade chooses its owner. Is that philosophy simply an example of early humans' tendency to project spiritual consciousness onto inanimate objects? Or might ancient swordsmiths like Amakuni really have possessed some otherworldly knowledge? A knowledge that swords, like other deadly weapons, come not from humans, but from a divine or extraterrestrial origin?

JOAN OF ARC AND KING ARTHUR

From fifteenth-century France comes another tale of a magical sword with extraordinary origins. When Joan of Arc was arrested and brought to her condemnation trial, her inquisitors were obsessed with finding out about her sword. It was supposed to have divine power. Joan claimed that angelic voices led her to it. It is said that the sword was forged by Saint Michael the Archangel and that whoever possessed it was invincible. That was true when Joan of Arc used her sword in the Battle of Orleans, a decisive battle that sparked the series of events that eventually put King Charles VII on the throne of France.

Ancient Astronaut theorists suggest that Joan of Arc might have been led to her invincible sword by extraterrestrials who had an interest in the future of France. They point to the story of King Arthur, a legendary British ruler of the late fifth and early sixth centuries, as evidence of that idea.

King Arthur had two swords, though in movies sometimes the famous Sword in the Stone and Excalibur are treated as one and the same. The Sword in the Stone was what it sounds like: a sword embedded in a boulder. Only the true king would be able to pull it out, as King Arthur did.

Giorgio Tsoukalos has an intersting theory about how that worked:

When I hear a story about this magnificent sword that's encased in this stone, with only the handle sticking out, and only King Arthur has the capability to pull it out, well then I start thinking about some type of a biometric security system, where today we now have guns that can only be fired if the handle recognizes your fingerprint. Is it possible that the sword in the stone was calibrated specifically to King Arthur's biometrics? I think yes.

Replica of King Arthur's legendary sword Excalibur

Statue of Joan of Arc in Paris, France

King Arthur's weapon was the legendary Excalibur, which came to him from the Lady in the Lake, whose hand came up and presented him with the magical sword. It shone with the light of thirty suns and blinded his enemies! Yet another magical sword? Or advanced technology that was misunderstood?

THE BLAZING POWER OF GREEK FIRE

In one battle in 941 AD, Prince Igor of Kiev attacked Constantinople with a fleet of 1,000 ships. Only five ships survived; the others were destroyed by Greek Fire.

Few knew the formula for Greek Fire even in the old days. Clearly it was a potent mix of incendiary chemicals. The most amazing thing is that scientists haven't been able to reproduce it. Experts think it must have been some kind of petroleum, or something involving phosphorous and magnesium, which can explode when mixed with water. But where did the secret recipe come from?

Roman Emperor Constantine is said to have been given the secret to this weapon by angels. In the sky, he witnessesed what he described as a cross hovering above him. He interpreted the vision as a sign from the Christian God. But was the cross-shaped object in the sky really a sign from God? Might it have been some other extraordinary force? An aircraft with straight wings could look like a cross, too. Is it possible that Constantine, instead of actually having seen a cross floating in the sky, saw some kind of extraterrestrial craft? Could Greek Fire have been a type of advanced alien technology given to Constantine to ensure the success of the Roman Empire?

Eleventh century depiction of Greek Fire

DID E.T. GIVE US GUNPOWDER?

While mixing chemicals in search of cures and even the key to immortality, alchemists in China as early as the year 850 AD came upon a mixture that made a real bang: gunpowder. Used in weapons such as cannons and primitive grenades, the booming powder helped China win battle after battle.

Gunpowder is made of charcoal, possibly from burnt trees, and sulfur, which could be obtained from volcanoes. It also needs potassium nitrate, a mineral that can come from caves. How did chemists of the time know how to mix these into such a potent cocktail? Could the formula for gunpowder have extraterrestrial origins? And if deadly technologies like gunpowder and Greek Fire really were handed down to humans by an alien race—a question remains: why?

PRIMITIVE LIGHT SABERS AND LASER BEAMS

In Southeast Asia and Cambodia, we can see evidence of yet another strange weapon that seems to have come from outer space: the mythical sword of Preah Pisnokar. In Cambodian mythology, Preah Pisnokar is the son of a human man and a woman who came from the sky. Stories say he was taken to the sky world and taught the technology of the gods.

Legends have credited him as being the architect behind the world's largest religious shrine, Angkor Wat, which sits just north of Cambodia's Tonlé Sap Lake. Besides magnificent structures, Preah Pisnokar was said to have fashioned a sword that made him invincible in

Angkor Wat Temple, Cambodia

battle. It was thin as a feather and could cut stone. Legend says that Preah Pisnokar threw his mighty weapon into the Tonlé Sap Lake when it grew too weak for him to use anymore. But how does a sword grow weak? According to Ancient Astronaut theorists, the blade had lost its power because it was made of light. What could they mean by "light"? At this time, fire was the only type of artificial light available. A sword of fire? That would be interesting, but what if it really was a sword made of light? This type of weapon is not unimaginable. Think about light sabers, for example. Might it one day be possible to create a weapon made of light? .

Ancient Astronaut theorists think it might have been some sort of laser beam, which is intensely focused light, or a plasma beam, which is energetically charged particles. For those theorists, descriptions of laser-type technology can be found in numerous texts throughout the ancient world. In China, there is a Yin-Yang mirror, which could kill opponents with a beam of light. The Maori god defeated rebels with a kind of laser-lightning weapon. In ancient India, the arrow of Brahma could have been some kind of laser weapon. Even Archimedes famously used some kind of magic mirror to create a laser that set ships on fire.

OTHERWORLDLY WARFARE OF INDIAN LEGEND

Today, unmanned aerial "drones" patrol skies around the world and undertake missions impossible or too dangerous for human pilots. Strangely, devices like these are described in texts more than 2,200 years old.

The Mahabharata, a sacred Hindu text, contains stories about epic battles in the sky among what were believed to be gods. In all, forty-six different types of weapons are described, including flying chariots, unmanned aircraft, and what can honestly be called weapons of mass destruction. Vishnu was said to wield incendiary weapons that could locate their targets, as if they could detect motion, or act like heat-seeking missiles. The Pashupatastra is a weapon that multiplies into seven different arrows and then hits seven targets. Salva, an anti-god, could make his vehicle disappear—like a stealth fighter.

Drone aircraft launching a missile

Probably the scariest device in those ancient epics was one called Brahmastra (Brahma's weapon), which Ancient Astronaut theorists believe could have been a sort of nuclear bomb of extraterrestrial origin. In the stories, people were burned and melted by the Brahma weapon, and descriptions of its deadly aftereffects are similar to the effects of exposure to intense radiation. One reference speaks of explosions brighter than a thousand suns, and that following these blasts, the suns were twirling in the air and trees went up in flames. Then people who survived lost their hair and their nails started to fall out. The similarities between these effects and those of radiation poisoning as seen after the United States dropped the world's first atomic bombs on Japanese cities during World War II, are uncanny. Could the description of the Brahma weapon actually be an earlier, extraterrestrial version of the nuclear bomb?

In 1922, an officer with an Indian archaeological survey group discovered the ruins of an ancient city known as Mohenjo-daro. Mainstream archaeologists say the city, whose name might have meant "mound of the dead," flourished between 2600 and 1900 BC. However, scientists in Pakistan have suggested Mohenjo-daro is much older. And later, in a 1979 book, *Atomic Destruction in 2000 B.C.*, British researcher David Davenport claimed to have found a fifty-yard-wide epicenter at Mohenjo-daro, where everything appeared to have been fused together as though heated and melted at an ultrahot temperature.

How is it that some of the earliest written accounts of warfare describe sophisticated weaponry that humans wouldn't develop for thousands of years?

Giorgio Tsoukalos thinks these tales weren't just made up.

I refuse to think that our ancestors came up with these stories out of thin air. When writing was first invented, they wrote down their history. The first things that were ever written down were actual events.

Ruins of the ancient city
Mohenjo-daro, in Sindh, Pakistan

What do the monsters of myths and legends—from Loch Ness Monster to Bigfoot to the three-headed dog Cerberus—have to do with aliens? Ancient Aliens theorists believe there may be a connection between these terrifying beasts and the idea that beings from beyond the Earth have visited us. How? One theory says aliens came to Earth to experiment and created fantastical and mutant creatures, just as our own scientists experiment with things like DNA, gene splicing, and transplantation of body parts with the aim of advancing medicine.

Today's genetic scientists and medical researchers are performing pioneering work in laboratories with "chimeras," organisms that have human cells and animal cells in their bodies. The results of these important experiments could help scientists better understand diseases, improve organ transplants, and test medicines. In 1954, a Russian scientist named Vladimir Demikhov—some might say a mad scientist—once transplanted a second dog's head onto a dog, as part of his research into organ transplants. In 2003, a scientist in China fused human skin cells with rabbit eggs to try to grow tissues that could be used in human patients. Genetic experiments like these are ongoing. Transplanting animal organs into people for medical purposes is called xenotransplantation.

The scientific term "chimera" actually dates back to Greek mythology and one of the oldest books that has survived from ancient times. In *The Iliad*, epic poet Homer describes the chimera as "a thing of immortal make, not human, lion-fronted and snake behind, a goat in the middle, and snorting out the breath of the terrible flame of bright fire."

Maybe our civilization's mythological beasts, many of which combine parts of various animals, really did exist—created by alien races that saw the Earth as a research lab filled with animals whose pieces could be mixed and matched!

Says Giorgio Tsoukalos:

If today we're able to create a two-headed dog with six legs, is it possible that a similar creature existed thousands of years ago? I say yes.

What do you think? Here are some strange and legendary beasts.

FAMOUS CHIMERAS AND HYBRID MONSTERS

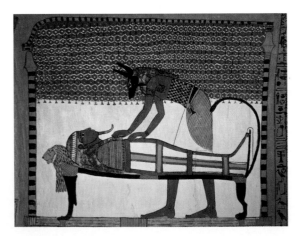

Cerberus

Hybrid beasts that combine different animals (or mix animals with people!) are part of many ancient mythologies. Written descriptions of extraordinary beasts and carvings and statues of them are found all around the world. Could these mixed-up creatures have been the results of breeding or genetic experiments by alien mad scientists? Could they be aliens themselves?

Cerberus was a three-headed dog of ancient Greek myth.

The Egyptian god Anubis had the body of a man with the head of a dog or jackal.

The legendary Naga from India were part man, part snake.

The Greek monster Medusa had a hairdo made of snakes.

Medusa

Pegasus was a flying white stallion with a bird's wings.

The ancient Greek centaur had the body of a horse and the head and upper body of a man.

The ancient Greek creature Minotaur had the head of a bull on the body of a man.

Painting of Anubis and a mummy (1314 to 1200 BC)

THE STORY OF GARUDA

In the middle of the Indus River Valley in southern Pakistan lie the ruins of Mohenjo-daro, an ancient city whose name means "mound of the dead." It was one of the largest urban settlements in the world in 2600 BC. Ancient Astronaut theorists think long ago it was the epicenter of some kind of devastating nuclear explosion. According to the Mahabharata—the ancient holy text of the Hindus—a white-hot smoke rose and reduced an ancient city to ashes. Some believe the ancient city it references is Mohenjo-daro. Horses were burned and corpses were vaporized by intense heat. Some skeletons found in modern times reportedly had far-above-normal radioactive levels, suggesting some kind of atomic blast occurred.

And, according to the ancient texts, a fearsome flying monster appeared in the sky after the devastation. It was called Garuda. Garuda was a huge birdlike creature with a red face, red wings, and sharp talons. The god Vishnu was said to ride on it.

Or was it something else? Some Ancient Astronaut theorists think Garuda may not have been a mutant beast. In some texts, Garuda's exterior isn't feathers—but metal. Maybe this ancient giant flying "beast" was actually a flying vehicle.

Statue of Garuda

MONSTERS IN THE WATER

The waters have given us many legendary monsters of mysterious origin. According to Scandinavian legend, gigantic sea monsters known as Kraken roamed the seas off the coasts of Norway and Greenland. They fiercely attacked ships, and when they submerged they created deadly whirlpools that could pull a ship down. In some legends, the Kraken is over a mile long, with hundreds of octopus-like arms. Could Kraken have actually existed, and does a story from the Bible offer clues to the origin of sea monsters?

In a famous Bible story, Jonah is at sea on a ship, after defying a command from God. A giant storm ensues, and when the crew throws Jonah overboard, the storm ends. Jonah is swallowed by a giant fish or whale that God has provided, and he spends three days inside, so the story goes. Eventually the whale spits Jonah onto dry land.

But was this whale a real, biological animal? Giorgio Tsoukalos says that in some references, you can read that the ribs of this whale were made out of gleaming bronze. That makes it sound like a vessel made of metal. Maybe Jonah was swallowed, not by a whale, but by a USO—an Unidentified Submersible Object!

No lineup of unexplained underwater monsters would be complete without the Loch Ness Monster. In the Highlands of Scotland, "Nessie" has long been part of Celtic and Norse folklore. Recorded accounts of sightings go back to the year 565 AD, to the Irish monk Saint Columba, who had his own run-in with Nessie, in which the beast came after him only to retreat after Columba defended himself. It's been reported that there have been UFO sightings over the Loch, too—of strange, brightly lit objects hovering over the water, late at night, vehicles that aren't helicopters or other aircraft.

WHAT ABOUT BIGFOOT?

Legends of large beasts that lurk in the wild—creatures that seem to be part ape, part man—come from all over the world. Hikers and explorers have reported fleeting glimpses and really big humanlike footprints, double the size of a human foot. In Asia, there's the legendary Abominable Snowman, or Yeti. In Australia, they speak of the Yowie. In North America, we have Bigfoot, also known as Sasquatch. He stands six to ten feet tall. He's hairy and, by many accounts, smelly. And very elusive.

But what makes anyone think Bigfoot is connected to aliens?

Ancient stories describe all kinds of encounters with apemanlike beasts. Viking explorer Leif Ericson in the tenth century wrote of "horrible, ugly, hairy creatures with dark eyes." In the remains of the ancient city of Nineveh, Sumerian tablets dating back to as early as 700 BC tell the story of King Gilgamesh, whose companion Enkudu is described as a hairy wild man living outside human society. Some Ancient Aliens proponents even believe that the giant Goliath from the Bible story of David and Goliath may be an early representation of a Bigfoot.

These same Ancient Aliens theorists believe that long ago aliens may have come to Earth to tinker with our species, possibly creating these hairy man-ape hybrids.

Some Sasquatch researchers have noted there's a connection between Bigfoot activity and UFO activity—reports happening in the same areas. There was a wave of UFO activity in Penn-

Artist's rendering of the Loch Ness Monster

Image of what a UFO might look like, according to many reports

sylvania in the early 1970s, and people also were reporting shadowy, lumbering apelike creatures walking out of the woods. Author and UFOlogist Linda Moulton Howe says she received a report from a man in Washington State who saw a silver disk in the sky, a beam coming down from it, and a shaggy gorilla-like man emerging.

THE MONTAUK MONSTER—MODERN DAY EVIDENCE?

In the summer of 2008 in Montauk, New York, a twenty-six-year-old woman and three of her friends discovered the carcass of a strange-looking dead creature that had washed onto the shore. It looked like a dog in some ways, but it had a beak like a bird, claws like a raccoon, and sharp teeth. It came to be called the Montauk Monster, and it remains unexplained today. Ancient Alien proponents believe the bizarre animal could be part of a long line of genetically modified creatures that have appeared throughout human history.

ALIENS AND THE OLD WEST

When you think about the days of America's Old West—the period during the 1800s when pioneers were moving westward and setting up towns—you might imagine cowboys and Indians, gunslingers and sheriffs drawing their six-shooters, whiskey bottles sliding across the bar in rowdy saloons. But visitors from outer space? Intergalactic spaceships that buzzed down to Earth while desperados were rustling cattle and robbing stagecoaches?

It's hard to believe, but several accounts from that early time in America's westward expansion describe events that remain mysterious.

"People were seeing things in the sky they couldn't explain," says Logan Hawkes, a magazine editor and researcher who wrote *Ancient Aliens of the Americas*. "The truth of the matter is there's some very interesting and incredible stories that come from the 1800s about flying objects and strange encounters and events."

As American pioneers were exploring the western frontier, there may have been another explorer checking in, from a far more distant frontier.

The Old West is rich in tales of mystery and extraterrestrial contact

EVIDENCE FILE: AURORA, TEXAS

Not far from modern-day Dallas is the town of Aurora, Texas. It was here in April of 1897—fifty years before the U.S. Army announced that a flying disk crashed in Roswell, New Mexico—that an unidentified flying object was reported to have crashed on the property of a local judge. Supposedly the strange airship smashed into a windmill and was mostly obliterated.

"The ship exploded in flame and was burnt to a crisp essentially," says Jeff Danelek, author of *The Great Airship of 1897*. "A local reporter arrived on the scene and he reported that there was a large debris field, and also that there was the charred remains of what appeared to be . . . an alien from another planet."

Most of what is known about the incident comes from the report that appeared in the *Dallas Morning News* on April 19, 1897. Part of the article said:

> The pilot of the ship is supposed to be the only one on board, and while his remains are badly disfigured, enough of the original has been picked up to show that he was not an inhabitant of this world.
>
> Mr. T. J. Weems, a United States signal service officer and an authority on astronomy, gives it as his opinion that he was a native of the planet Mars. Papers found on this person—evidently the record of his travels—are written in some unknown hieroglyphics, and cannot be deciphered.

A Windmill Demolishes It.

Aurora, Wise Co., Tex.,April 17.—(To The News.)—About 6 o'clock this morning the early risers of Aurora were astonished at the sudden appearance of the airship which has been sailing through the country.

It was traveling due north, and much nearer the earth than ever before. Evidently some of the machinery was out of order, for it was making a speed of only ten or twelve miles an hour and gradually settling toward the earth. It sailed directly over the public square, and when it reached the north part of town collided with the tower of Judge Proctor's windmill and went to pieces with a terrific explosion, scattering debris over several acres of ground, wrecking the windmill and water tank and destroying the judge's flower garden.

The pilot of the ship is supposed to have been the only one on board, and while his remains are badly disfigured, enough of the original has been picked up to show that he was not an inhabitant of this world. Mr. T. J. Weems, the United States signal service officer at this place and an authority on astronomy, gives it as his opinion that he was a native of the planet Mars. Papers found on his person—evidently the record of his travels—are written in some unknown hieroglyphics, and can not be deciphered.

The ship was too badly wrecked to form any conclusion as to its construction or motive power. It was built of an unknown metal, resembling somewhat a mixture of aluminum and silver, and it must have weighed several tons.

The town is full of people to-day who are viewing the wreck and gathering specimens of the strange metal from the debris. The pilot's funeral will take place at noon to-morrow.

S. E. HAYDON.

Newspaper article suggesting UFO activity in Aurora, Texas, skies

The ship was too badly wrecked to form any conclusion as to its construction or motive power. It was built of an unknown metal, resembling somewhat a mixture of aluminum and silver, and it must have weighed several tons.

Back in those days, manned travel in hot-air balloons existed, so the idea of an airship floating across the sky wasn't completely unheard of. But 1897 "was six years before the Wright Brothers actually made heavier-than-air craft work," according to UFO researcher Jim Marrs. So what could this mystery machine actually have been?

Witnesses claimed that debris from the crash was recovered by local law enforcement officials and never seen again. Others claim that the judge buried bits of the wreckage at the bottom of a deep well. The incident was mostly forgotten for decades until, in 1945, a man named Brawley Oates, who had purchased the land, blamed his severe case of arthritis on contaminated, maybe radioactive, water from the well.

Who or what was the strange aircraft's pilot? The body reportedly was taken to the Aurora Cemetery after the crash and buried there, creating a new source of mystery and controversy that continues to this day. After the 1947 Ros-well incident began stirring curiosity, some researchers began a move to exhume the remains of the pilot's body—that is, dig it up to see if any new clues about it could be uncovered. Officials denied the requests to dig at the site. Jim Marrs says the small tombstone that once marked the burial location of the pilot went missing. But he knew where it was, and in 1973, he and newspaper reporter Bill Case got a metal detector and found three readings

Tombstone featuring the carving of a UFO from the Aurora Cemetery

of metal at the gravesite. When they returned later, there were no metal readings—but holes had been drilled as if someone had extracted something. No one claimed to have tampered with anything.

Today, the Texas State Historical Commission has a marker at the cemetery discussing the story of the crash and the legend that an extraterrestrial pilot may have been buried there long ago. But what really happened remains a mystery.

✳ INCIDENT REPORT: GREAT FALLS, MONTANA

October 19, 1865. Six months after the tragic assassination of President Abraham Lincoln, a fur trapper reports what might be the first documented UFO crash in the Old West. According to the *Missouri Democrat*, the trapper observed a light flying through the sky over his camp and crashing in a nearby forest. When he tracked it down, he found a large stone embedded in the side of a mountain. The stone was cracked and hollow. According to the newspaper account, inside were hieroglyphic markings. The area along the upper Missouri River was home to the Blackfoot Indians, whose folklore told of alien visitations.

"The Blackfoot have very profound legends and myths relating to beings, which quite clearly are said to have come down from some kind of sky world to earth and in these sky vehicles," says Andrew Collins, author of *The Cygnus Mystery*. "And the way that they are described, these can be modern ideas of flying saucers or UFOs."

Could the object that the Montana fur trapper claimed to have found have been one of the alien crafts described in Blackfoot legends?

UNEXPLAINED FLYING OBJECTS: THUNDERBIRDS AND FLYING BEASTS?

The town of Tombstone, in southern Arizona near Tucson, is renowned as the location of the gunfight at the O.K. Corral, the 1881 shootout in which Deputy Town Marshal Wyatt Earp and Doc Holliday took on the notorious Clanton gang. Less than ten years later, it would become the location of one of the most bizarre UFO sightings in history.

Explains John Whalen, author of *The Big Book of the Weird Wild West*: "According to a story in the

Figurine of a flying beast, known as a Thunderbird

Tombstone Epitaph in 1890, two ranchers were out in the desert of Arizona when they saw some sort of monstrous bird flying overhead with a huge wingspan. The body was described as being like an alligator, and the wings were described as membranous." They supposedly shot at it, but weren't able to harm it.

That wasn't the only reported Old West sighting of an extraordinary creature flying across the sky.

Located in California, Elizabeth Lake was called Laguna del Diablo—the Devil's Lake—by Mexican settlers who came

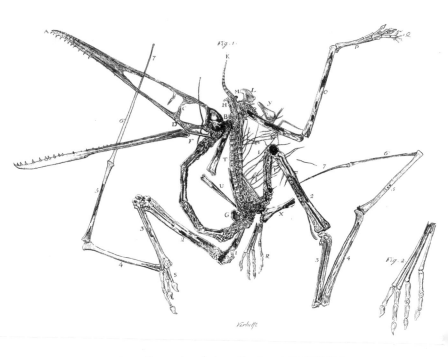

According to descriptions, the Thunderbird might have looked something like this ancient pterodactyl.

to the area long ago. Legend said the devil's own pet would enter this world through a hole at the bottom of the lake, which was supposed to be a portal to the underworld. Geologically the lake is above the infamous San Andreas fault line (an area known for extreme, violent, and ground-splitting earthquakes), lending credence to this theory. From about the 1800s onward, landowners who built around the lake claimed to have been visited by some sort of flying beast. Some called it a Thunderbird and described it similarly to what had been reported in Tombstone.

Were people really seeing a species of strange, large birds that no person had ever encountered before? Or might it be possible that the Thunderbird wasn't a creature at all? Were these loud, large flying things really birds, or could they have been a form of sophisticated flying technology?

Native Americans knew what real birds looked like, says Erich von Däniken, the pioneering author of *Chariots of the Gods*. "But now something different arrived," he says. "An object which could fly, which is bigger than the eagle, but at the same time makes tremendous noise. So you have the creation of the Thunderbird."

Did the cowboys in Tombstone, Arizona, and ranchers at Elizabeth Lake witness extraterrestrial ships that may have been visiting North America for thousands of years?

Left: portrait of Ambrose Bierce Right: portrait of Edgar Allan Poe, from whom Bierce drew inspiration for his stories

VANISHING VISIONARY: AMBROSE BIERCE

The Civil War veteran Ambrose Bierce was one of the great early American short story writers. Bierce also believed in the possibility of life beyond our world, and his death—really his *disappearance*—has never been explained.

Bierce is most famous for writing a thrilling short story called "An Occurrence at Owl Creek Bridge," which later was made into an episode of the classic sci-fi TV show *The Twilight Zone*. It's about a Civil War soldier who is being hung as a traitor. Somehow he escapes from the hangman's noose at the last possible moment and makes a daring escape.

Another Bierce story involves a bizarre disappearance. In "The Difficulty of Crossing a Field," an Alabama farmer in 1854 is walking across a field when—poof!—he is gone.

Bierce seems to have been influenced by Edgar Allan Poe's stories of mystery, science, and horror, and also by Native American folklore. In addition to belief in star beings, some Native Americans believed in the existence of interdimensional gateways or portals, which would enable visitors to travel between time and space. Still, the strangeness connected with Ambrose Bierce might have ended in his fantastical writing—but Bierce seemed intent on discovering something for himself.

In the early 1900s, he is believed to have ventured into Mexico, to an area known for strange phenomena, called Paquime. The Tarahumara, a Paquime tribe, are known for their visions of star beings. Paquime is in the same region as the Crystal Cave, where the largest crystal deposits in the world are found. Bierce may have ventured there with Frederick Albert Mitchell-Hedges, a British adventurer known for his discovery of a Mayan crystal skull, which he believed could have been a way to communicate with extraterrestrial beings. Where did Bierce go? His last known communication was a letter in which he wrote: "I leave tomorrow for an unknown destination." Where the great writer's final destination was—just like the farmer in his story—to this day remains unknown.

CONCLUSION

Ancient Astronaut theorists examine and reexamine historical events for signs of ancient alien contact missed by archaeologists and historians throughout history. They piece together evidence and look for obvious connections between our civilizations and those of other worlds, often culminating in compelling findings.

In this past century alone, humans were able to blast off from our home and touch the stars and planets beyond. We sent satellites into orbit, landed on the moon, and reached Mars with machines imagined and created in laboratories. These quests were not approached with closed minds, but with thoughts and dreams of what might be beyond the sky. Is there something else out there? Or better yet, someone else?

Perhaps our first attempts to travel into the depths of space, to communicate with the unknown civilizations that surely populate foreign planets, have been seen as a signal to whoever is out there. Perhaps after centuries of writing on cave walls, building pyramids, and charting the skies, other civilizations are ready to make contact with us again. Maybe they were just waiting for us.

Our universe is big—bigger than we can comprehend—and it's full of mysteries that have yet to be solved. Were our ancestors really capable of the incredible achievements within this book, or might they have had help from another source, one older and wiser than us?

The questions are always there: Has life on Earth been influenced by alien encounters from the very beginning? What influence might these encounters with extraterrestrials have had on the outcome of human history? And most important, when will they visit us next?

EXAMINING THE EVIDENCE: VIEWING ACTIVITY

I. View a clip or full episode of *Ancient Aliens* online at www.history.com/shows/ancient-aliens or on DVD (visit www.history.com/shop to purchase, also available on iTunes).

2. Locate the area(s) in the clip or episode on a map to have a sense of the geographical region covered.

3. Answer the questions below and discuss your thoughts and responses.

What time periods and places are explored in this clip?

What is one new thing you learned about this culture or historic site?

Which theories or findings in this clip or episode did you find most interesting?

What kinds of sources would you use to learn more about this topic?

4. Write an essay or a letter to a friend compiling the information above and drawing together your arguments. Do you find Ancient Astronaut theory to be plausible?

LEARN MORE:

Visit www.history.com/shows/ancient-aliens to watch video clips and learn more about *Ancient Aliens*.

PICTURE CREDITS

i-ii: Albert Ziganshin/Shutterstock; v: NASA; 2: Shutterstock; 3: John Arnold/Superstock; 4: Prometheus Entertainment; 5: National Archives and Records Administration; 6–7 background: Shutterstock; 8: Ton Koene/Superstock; 10–11: (left to right): Steve Whiston /Superstock, Prometheus Entertainment, LACMA- www.lacma.org, Superstock, De Agostini/ A. Dogli Oriti—Getty Images; 13: NASA; 14: NASA; 15: NASA; 16: Shutterstock; 17 background: NASA; 18–19: iurii/Shutterstock; 20: sacredtexts.com/public domain (India and US); 21: Superstock; 22: National Geographic Image Collection; 23: Superstock; 24: Prometheus Entertainment; 25: Library of Congress public domain; 26: Shutterstock; 27: NASA; 28: Fine Art Images/Superstock; 29: F1 ONLINE/Superstock; Photononstop/ Superstock; 30–31: National Geographic Stock Images; 32: Iryna 1/Shutterstock; 33: Hans P. Szyszka/Novarc/Corbis; 34–35: fstockfoto/Shutterstock; 36–37: Alberto Loyo/Shutterstock; 38: National Geographic Image Collection/Alamy; 40–41: Fulcanelli/ Shutterstock; 42–43: Christina Rutz; 44: AridOcean/Shutterstock; 45, 46: Dmitry Burlakov/Shutterstock; 47: David Hlavacek/Shutterstock; 48–49: National Geographic Stock Images; 51: Prometheus Entertainment; 52: NASA/JPL-Caltech/IRAS /H. McCallon; 53: Kokhanchikov/Shutterstock; 54: Manamana/Shutterstock; 56: chasethestorm.com/ Shutterstock; 57: A&E Television Network; 59: Christian Musat/Shutterstock; 62: Joze Pojbic/Getty Images; 63: A&E Television Network; 65: Nemequene- Wikimedia_Quimbaya; 67: NASA; 68: Linda Bucklin/ Shutterstock; 69: William Scott-Elliott; 71: Elena Yakusheva/ Shutterstock; 72: JTB Media Creation, inc./ Alamy; 74: Georgios Kollidas/ Shutterstock; 75: Anton Ivanov/ Shutterstock; 77: Prometheus Entertainment; 78: Shutterstock; 79: De Agostini/ A. Dogli Oriti—Getty Images; 80: Royal Armouries, Leeds, UK / Bridgeman Images; 81: Fer Gregory/ Shutterstock; 82: Nikonaft/Shutterstock; 83: Fine Art Images/ Superstock; 84: James Wheeler/ Shutterstock; 85: Paul Fleet/ Shutterstock; 86: James L. Stanfield/National Geographic Creative; 87: NASA; 88 (left to right): Malchev/Shutterstock, Bridgeman Art Library/ Superstock; Shutterstock; 89: Thewada1976/Shutterstock; 90: Victor Habbick/ Shutterstock; 92: Ursatii/Shutterstock; 93: National Geographic Stock Images; 94: S.E. Hayden, 1897, *The Dallas Morning News*; 95: Lori D. Martin; 96: Prometheus Entertainment; 97: Wellnhofer; 98: John Herbert Evelyn Partington; unknown; 100–101: Photobank Gallery/ Shutterstock

INDEX